"Krista and James White have created the blueprint for how to use the best design-thinking principles in the area where they should have been used in the first place: our people. Get your digital device or Moleskine notebook, buckle your seatbelt, open the book, and get to work."

—**MICHAEL C. BUSH,** Global CEO, Great Place to Work; author, *A Great Place to Work for All*

"Together, Krista and James White take the conversation to a new level, offering innovative ideas and insights. Their perspectives are completely different yet perfectly aligned around a shared purpose. I have seen firsthand how their steady guidance has supported multiple CEOs—they are, without question, exceptional leaders. *Culture Design* is a reflection of that wisdom."

—**JESSICA ALBA,** founder and Board Director, Honest Company

"In a world full of clichés and uninspired leadership advice, *Culture Design* stands out with concrete, practical, and truly inspiring ways to build a durable culture. This book is essential reading, offering intentional strategies from both the vantage point of an iconic business leader and the fresh perspective of a next-generation entrepreneur."

—**MERLINE SAINTIL,** Lead Director, Rocket Lab; Board Director, Symbotic, TD Synnex, and GitLab

"Culture has never been more critical to business results, yet it remains an abstract topic for many CEOs. James and Krista White make culture pragmatic. More important, they help CEOs ensure they're creating the culture that their specific strategy and customer base requires. Highly recommended."

—**DAVID REIMER,** CEO, ExCo Group

"*Culture Design* is not only a fantastic guide for anyone in leadership but a valuable manual for investing in the culture of your team and organization. The coauthoring duo of James and Krista proves to be another valuable resource filled with multigenerational insight."

—**KECIA STEELMAN,** President and CEO, Ulta Beauty

"*Culture Design* is a powerful read full of excellent advice for companies and cultures of every size and industry. This dynamic father-daughter team brings new perspective to the age-old question of how to build culture at a time when society is undergoing rapid change. This book will inspire anyone who leads people—or aspires to lead people—to know, do, and measure what matters for the long-term success of their organizations."

—**RON SHAICH,** founder and former CEO, Panera Bread

"Krista and James White expertly illustrate how great company cultures get built through their 'Culture Stories from the Field' that make each chapter feel tangible for leaders' real lives. *Culture Design* is a must-read for any CEO, board, or executive team considering culture transformation."

—**KEITH MEYER,** Global Practice Leader, Board Services, Major, Lindsey & Africa

"Krista and James White personify leaders who lead by example and who inspire, motivate, and shape a culture that has meaning and longevity."

—**JUE WONG,** CEO, Performance Beauty Group

"*Culture Design* provides leaders with a straightforward process to build and sustain competitive advantage through culture. If all organizations were to follow these principles and steps, the value created for all organizational stakeholders would be immense."

—**AMY J. HILLMAN,** Rusty Lyon Chair of Strategy and former Dean, W. P. Carey School of Business, Arizona State University

Culture
Design

Culture Design

How to Build a
High-Performing,
Resilient Organization
with Purpose

James D. White
Krista White

HARVARD BUSINESS REVIEW PRESS
BOSTON, MASSACHUSETTS

HBR Press Quantity Sales Discounts

Harvard Business Review Press titles are available at significant quantity discounts when purchased in bulk for leadership development programs, client gifts, or sales promotions. Opportunities to co-brand copies with your logo or messaging are also available. For details and discount information for both print and ebook formats, contact booksales@hbr.org or visit www.hbr.org/bulksales.

Copyright 2025 James D. White and Krista White

All rights reserved

Printed in the United States of America

10 9 8 7 6 5 4 3 2 1

No part of this publication may be reproduced, stored in or introduced into a retrieval system, or transmitted, in any form, or by any means (electronic, mechanical, photocopying, recording, or otherwise), without the prior permission of the publisher. Requests for permission should be directed to permissions@harvardbusiness.org, or mailed to Permissions, Harvard Business School Publishing, 60 Harvard Way, Boston, Massachusetts 02163.

The web addresses referenced in this book were live and correct at the time of the book's publication but may be subject to change.

Library of Congress Cataloging-in-Publication Data

Names: White, James D., 1960- author. | White, Krista, author.
Title: Culture design : how to build a high-performing, resilient organization with purpose / James D. White, Krista White.
Description: Boston, Massachusetts : Harvard Business Review Press, [2025] | Includes bibliographical references and index.
Identifiers: LCCN 2025011475 (print) | LCCN 2025011476 (ebook) | ISBN 9798892790772 (hardcover ; alk. paper) | ISBN 9798892790789 (epub)
Subjects: LCSH: Corporate culture. | Leadership. | Organization.
Classification: LCC HD58.7 .W495 2025 (print) | LCC HD58.7 (ebook)
LC record available at https://lccn.loc.gov/2025011475
LC ebook record available at https://lccn.loc.gov/2025011476

ISBN: 979-8-89279-077-2
eISBN: 979-8-89279-078-9

The paper used in this publication meets the requirements of the American National Standard for Permanence of Paper for Publications and Documents in Libraries and Archives Z39.48-1992.

For Rose Marie, our beloved mother and Granny, who always encouraged us to shoot for the stars. We know the little woman with the big nose will always be sitting on our shoulders.

Contents

Introduction: Find Your Why　　　　　　　　　　　　　　1

Part One
Know What Matters

  1　Leaders Empathize　　　　　　　　　　　　　17
  2　Leaders Define the Reality　　　　　　　　　　45

Part Two
Do What Matters

  3　Leaders Work the Plan　　　　　　　　　　　　69
  4　Leaders Iterate　　　　　　　　　　　　　　　91
  5　Leaders Bring Culture to Life　　　　　　　　　111

Part Three
Measure What Matters

  6　Leaders Measure Progress　　　　　　　　　　131

Conclusion: Leaders Build a Future That Works for All　　155

Notes　　　　　　　　　　　　　　　　　　　　　173
Index　　　　　　　　　　　　　　　　　　　　　177
Acknowledgments　　　　　　　　　　　　　　　187
About the Authors　　　　　　　　　　　　　　　*191*

Preface

We started this project as a follow-up to our first book together, *Anti-Racist Leadership*, to do our part in igniting the change we wanted to see in the world and to bring hope and optimism to the topic of corporate culture. What follows is a father and daughter's love letter to the next generation of great leaders of companies built by design and on purpose.

Our original thesis then was about building a great corporate culture in a divided world on the backdrop of the pandemic, global supply chain disruptions, and the 2020 racial reckoning and US election. We thought we had reached the most chaos and turmoil we had ever experienced. But the environment we see today has only grown in its unpredictability and polarization.

For leaders, the world is literally burning around them, being upended by wars in Ukraine and Gaza and shifting politics worldwide. This includes the 2024 US presidential election, which, despite our experiences throughout the past eight years, managed to shock many, including us, with its divisiveness and outcome.

Despite the turbulent cultural and social changes worldwide, we are in awe of the steadfast, passionate, and empathetic leaders we were able to interview for this book, including old friends and generous

Preface

new colleagues. Our conversations have made us hopeful, and we are thrilled to share our learnings. We continue to be grateful for the opportunity to learn and grow together as father and daughter and lifelong learners. We hope to continue encouraging each other, and you, to stay curious, to always ask the most important question: *Why?*

Culture
Design

Introduction

Find Your Why

Whether you're a CEO being pulled in opposite directions by stakeholders, an HR leader working to break down siloes, or a middle manager spread too thin, you know this to be true: for better or worse, your company has a culture. It seems obvious, but it's important to say it. In any organization, a culture will emerge by default—without anyone doing anything other than being there. How would you describe your organization's culture? Are you happy with it? Do you think you fully understand it? Do you know the risks and opportunities your company culture creates?

Most importantly, have you done anything to shape or change that culture *by design*?

If you have, that's a good start. If you haven't, you must. It's time to get *intentional* about organizational culture and to make it strong on purpose. Strong company cultures, deliberately shaped, are the difference between businesses that are great versus those that are just good enough. And increasingly, strong company cultures make the difference between businesses that will thrive and those that won't.

The business world is at a crossroads. Organizations have been pulled into a divided, burning world and are expected to take stands, acknowledge their role in society, and face real economic and social consequences when they don't. Leaders are struggling to stay aligned to their true north while satisfying their employees, shareholders, and consumers. Gen Z has entered the workforce with new expectations as workers and consumers. AI is a looming specter in a tech sector already disrupted by mass layoffs.[1] Call it VUCA, call it permacrisis—whatever language makes most sense to you. The hard truth is that, in this climate, a weak culture will lead to a lack of trust and commitment from workers and customers. And a weak culture leads to weak results. Conversely, company cultures that focus on longevity, sustainability, and purpose provide a kind of armor against the precariousness of leading a company in this age.

Let's be clear: such a culture will not organically emerge. It will not come from giving your team free lunch and foosball tables. Declaring what your culture is and expecting it to be true holds no more water than that nebulous marketing cliché "satisfaction guaranteed." Yet leaders we consult with on culture design continually express all of these ideas. They treat culture like something they know is there but have little power over, or they look to fringe benefits to signal culture, or they project ideas and words about the culture that aren't aligned with behaviors and actions within the company. No amount of saying you value your employees' happiness, for example, will make that true if you're not *designing* your organization to value your employees' happiness. If anything, saying it and not living it makes matters much, much worse.

Introduction

You must approach culture *intentionally*. There's that word again. You'll see it a lot. It's one of the most important words in this book. We call this process *culture design*, and we want you to unlearn the belief that this work is an organic thing, a "soft" leadership topic you'll get to when you have time. It's not. It is—to repeat—the thing that will make your company thrive in an age when most factors are conspiring against your success.

Think about culture design in a material sense, like car design or shoe design. We're here to take the same kinds of practical, intentional steps you'd take when building a great product. We're here to do the work, to teach you how to intentionally design a culture that is resilient, inclusive, powerful, and effective.

But what even *is* culture? You'll get a different answer from every person you ask. Veteran marketing executive and board member Tony Wells called culture "the software that makes companies achieve business outcomes"; while Advantage Solutions CEO Dave Peacock made the point that "culture is caught, not taught."[2]

We define organizational culture as a set of actions, habits, rituals, and beliefs that determine how work gets done, how decisions get made, and how people experience their workplaces.

This is the definition we use in our coaching and consulting practice, Culture Design Lab. Founded in 2020, it is an extension of the work James has done throughout his whole career. James has thirty-plus years of experience as an operating executive and a deep knowledge of the consumer products, retail, and restaurant industries. Additionally, he has spent twenty years in the boardroom across various industry sectors. His perspective is that of an operating executive who has always been focused on putting people first and building high-performing teams. He gets his direct, no-nonsense approach to

Introduction

coaching from his upbringing by hardworking Midwestern parents. Cutting through the fat is integral to his focus on organizational culture and informs much of the tone we're setting here about this being a real, operational imperative. From day one, he has striven to be an inclusive leader whose job is to bring out the best in everyone. He sees culture as something that must be embedded from the top down and bottom up, with a strong focus on middle management as the hinge to maximize a company's potential.

Krista is a writer and founder. She recently graduated with her MFA in fiction. She is also the founder of Kiki For The Future, an app that curates sex education resources for the LGBTQIA+ community. Her connection to the work of organizational culture is through the lens of creating a better, more equitable, and freer world for all. She sees business as a tool to improve people's lives through purpose, enjoyment, and wealth creation. She believes that it isn't a radical idea to suggest that people should enjoy their jobs, especially considering how much of our lives we spend at work. She also believes businesses should be a force for good not only for their employees but for the world around them. After all, their employees live in the communities that companies serve. She brings a storytelling lens to the work and aims to distill James's decades of practical experience into an easily digestible and practical framework for culture design.

By teaming up, we bring James's strong point of view driven by his operating experience across sectors and years in the boardroom—balanced, fortified, and pressure-tested by Krista's millennial eye and a perspective on which leaders are best suited to build cultures that work for all. James brings the executive's point of view; Krista, the worker's. James is from an established generation; Krista's generation is part of the emerging core of most businesses' workforces.

Introduction

These differences are a major asset to creating a framework for culture design. We come together on this work and combine our expertise and unique perspectives on this topic by embracing tension and staying open to each other's ideas. We debate. We don't always agree, but we always agree to listen and learn from each other, and it's made our work stronger, both at the Culture Design Lab and in what you'll learn in this book.

Ultimately the sum is greater than the parts because we are both driven by a shared love for building great companies led by people-first leaders. We've always thought about this work from a design perspective that is flexible enough to adapt to many operational models—there is no one-size-fits-all solution to the complex problems companies face. We are a catalyst for positive change for companies, and we've worked in a variety of modes in our consulting work—from helping large organizations think about transforming their entire company culture, to facilitating a discussion with a loss-prevention team inside a company on representation and bias, to coaching a CEO or board through a change agenda that requires focus around building a high-performance team and a stronger culture.

It's fair to ask why our consulting firm needs to exist if we can all agree that culture is the key that unlocks a new level of employee satisfaction and retention, productivity, innovation, and growth. You'd be hard-pressed to find someone who disagrees in spirit with these ideas, so why isn't everyone successfully investing in great cultures?

Part of the problem is what we alluded to before, a mismatch between actions and words—what Tony Wells calls the "say/do gap."[3] Leaders create beautiful, well-written documents outlining their mission, values, and purpose, only to stop short of backing up their words with actions. Creating the intention will always only be a starting point. The real work is in bringing culture to life in every action, decision, and behavior within the organization. This requires a mindset shift that's far more difficult to implement than a poster espousing certain values. In our experience, the crux of the disconnect comes when leaders treat culture like a task, a check-the-box activity. It is an iterative process that must be owned and *lived* by the CEO and senior leadership team. Using what we've gleaned working with clients, talking to dozens of business leaders, as well as James's operational experience, we have developed the Culture Design framework to help them—help you—get past the task-oriented notion of culture and start to build something more meaningful and lasting. **Culture Design is a foundational process by which design thinking principles are integrated with inclusive leadership best practices to build human, empathetic, and high-performing cultures suited to the needs of each organization.**

This book shows you how to implement it.

Culture Design is not an academic framework but rather an operational way of thinking about organizational culture. Both the name of our company and the way we work with this framework were inspired by design thinking principles. James took a deep dive into design thinking as a Stanford Distinguished Careers Institute fellow in 2018, and he's been reflecting on how its tenets apply to businesses and organizational culture ever since. Krista forayed into design thinking through UX design courses at General Assembly in New York, where she applied the concept to found her company and create the Kiki For The Future app.

Our understanding of designing corporate culture includes our own remix of the design thinking process, which works particularly well due to its human-centric, collaborative, and adaptive nature. It would be

Introduction

disingenuous to say that we sat down and followed this process to the letter every day for decades. Rather, it is a responsive way to make sense of the learned and intuited culture best practices we've uncovered.

For our purposes of culture design, we will divide the design thinking process into three parts, reflected in the three sections of this book. Part 1, "Know What Matters," lays the foundation by explaining the behaviors you need to start embracing to be an intentional designer of culture. In chapter 1, "Leaders Empathize," we'll explore the tools you can use to understand the needs, desires, and pain points of your workforce, customers, and other stakeholders. In chapter 2, "Leaders Define the Reality," we help you create an intentional vision for your future organization with prioritization frameworks that you will use to zero in on the high-impact issues and which actions to take to address them.

Part 2, "Do What Matters," will animate everything you learned in part 1. It is the practical heart of the book, the hammering of the steel and fastening with rivets. Chapter 3, "Leaders Work the Plan," shows you how to purposefully integrate culture to enable strategy execution and improve the long-term performance of the organization. Chapter 4, "Leaders Iterate," outlines the ways you can begin to deploy your culture design as a beta product and improve on it as you go and includes many case studies showing how other companies have done it. Chapter 5, "Leaders Bring Culture to Life," explores the step that is akin to product launch and will provide ways for you to engage middle managers and frontline workers to solidify and reinforce your culture design.

In part 3, "Measure What Matters," we focus on continuous improvement and sustaining your newly designed culture. Chapter 6, "Leaders Measure Progress," provides a method for taking stock of what data is currently being collected and how leaders can evaluate

Introduction

what needs to be measured to make their culture design succeed over the long term.

The conclusion, "Leaders Build a Future That Works for All," provides capstone learnings. It emphasizes the importance of legacy, sustainability, and sticking with culture design for the long haul, even when it requires standing alone. This is the clarion call to leaders to make culture design central to their job.

Notes from Krista and James

Throughout the book, both of us will be inserting individual insights. We've included two below, so you get a sense of them. We believe the book has a unified voice that comprises our shared point of view, but sometimes it helps to bring to life an idea, takeaways, anecdote, or counterpoint from one of us in isolation, and we thought this was the best way to demonstrate that. These asides also serve to emphasize how differing intergenerational voices can collaborate in harmony.

 ## From James's Notepad

I love working through a problem with good old-fashioned pen and paper. No need to reinvent the wheel! I'm also a visual learner, so having a notepad near me allows me to organize my thoughts with diagrams and drawings. The written notes that you'll see reflected in these asides are intended to provide an insider peek into the thought processes, learnings, and stories that drive me as an operational leader and a dad. My hope is

Introduction

that getting into the nitty-gritty will make designing culture on purpose feel as tangible as my notepad. I encourage you to keep one handy, too, while you read the book and while you do the work of designing your culture.

 From Krista's Notes App

You should see the notes app on my phone! Being able to search through all my thoughts and lists makes it easier for me to keep track of what's important. My notes are from a different perspective than Dad's and will be focused on my experiences as a small business owner and a frontline worker. I hope these notes open a different way of looking at things and connect to parts of your life that you may not have linked with organizational culture. You can use pen and paper if you want, but I suspect my peers will be tapping into their phones.

Start Here: What Is Your Why?

Before we get started, we urge you to do this exercise. It's something we do at the outset of all our engagements and something that we'll be referring back to constantly throughout the book, just as we would with a client on site.

Take a moment to consider your *why*. You may have heard about this concept from younger employees who not only want to be told *how* to work but *why* they're doing the work. It's become a popular refrain—even from young athletes who demand more from coaches than just being told where to line up and what to do. As a millennial, Krista is always thinking about the *why* behind our actions.

You should, too. James thinks of the question of "Why?" as fundamental to building companies both with the intentionality of culture design and through the importance of always connecting strategy and purpose. While there are numerous studies on the impact of building strong culture on the bottom line, we also encourage leaders to look beyond short-term profits to the long-term impact their organizations will have on their stakeholders and the world around them. Knowing what matters means both knowing what matters to *you* as much as it means knowing what matters to your organization. For both of us, this goes back to a focus on purpose in the workplace.

In her book *The Wake Up*, activist and DEI leader Michelle MiJung Kim dedicates a chapter to defining your why for wanting to build inclusive cultures. She writes, "The what is important, but without first understanding the why, the what and even the how eventually fall short of achieving sustainable change."[4] We are so quick to jump to solutions and actions that we rarely reflect on why the work we are doing matters. After the murder of George Floyd, people of color, especially Black folks (whether they specialized in DEI or not) were bombarded with questions like, "What can I do?" James received more calls than ever before from executives and board members ready to make a change; few mainstream businesspeople had previously even uttered the term *anti-racism* prior to 2020. But Kim makes a great point: take time for self-reflection before you act. Jumping directly into action can lead to stalled momentum and burnout.

Here, too, we ask you to reflect on why before diving into the work of building a strong, intentional company culture. In our work with clients, we see consistently that the folks best equipped to do the work of transforming culture are more broadly clear on their why. In writing this book, we spoke to leaders that we admired and are inspired by, all of whom bring to life best practices for designing great cultures, which across the board are always underpinned by a deeper why.

Furthermore, Kim states "When profit is the motive, then the efforts stop making sense when there is no clear threat of sustained financial loss or a major gain in the short term."[5] What Kim is suggesting here is that financial results alone are not the driver that sustains the work of culture transformation. It's not a why. Culture design takes time. Even if we're using the design thinking that's been applied to so many product designs and rollouts, transforming culture is not like launching a new iPhone—you won't see immediate returns. It's a months-long, even multiyear endeavor, and it will take time to see the fruits of your labor reflected in the bottom line. If you don't know your why and constantly reflect on it, you may lose faith if you're not seeing some kind of direct return right away. Those who know their why don't lose faith.

So, what is your deeper why for doing this work? Every company has a purpose beyond maximizing profits for its shareholders. And every leader should have a purpose beyond building their own wealth. You can make money anywhere. Why here? Why now? What motivates you to come to work every day? Do you *like* your job? The people you work with? We all deserve to do work that is fulfilling and meaningful in some way.

The idea of digging beneath profit to find a deeper why may feel counterintuitive to many leaders, who just want the practical advice: *Give me the framework. I know how to execute.* After all, bonuses, equity compensation, promotions, and job security are all tied to a company's economic performance. But leaders must learn to hold more than one truth at once. Profit matters, deeply. It is what makes a business a business to begin with. We aren't denying the importance of profit, of compensation, or of wealth creation. We are simply making the assertion that profit isn't the only important thing in a business. Furthermore, we're suggesting that putting people first can lead to record profits in the long term, even if that's difficult to see or believe now. There isn't an either/or. There is both/and.

Once you've taken the time to reflect and find your deeper why, you may feel stuck. Here are some prompts to help you gain clarity:

- What does your ideal world look like?

- How can your company fit into that vision for the world?

- What is currently working in your organization?

- Where is there room for improvement?

- How would your ideal world change your company and your life?

Take a few minutes to journal on the prompts above and write your why statement below.

> I want to embark on a culture transformation in my organization in order to _____. The impact this will have on me and my team is that _____.

We strongly encourage you to go through this exercise before moving on, and to keep it close by as you continue to read. We promise there's so much practical content coming to help you do culture design in a way that makes your company stronger. But none of it matters if you don't know your why.

And once you've written your why statement, use it as a guiding light as you embark on this work. Bookmark this page for when you need a reminder or when you want to revise your why statement. Keep coming back to it.

Okay. Let's get to work on an intentional culture design.

Guiding Questions

- At first glance, what needs to change about your organization's culture?

- Are you ready to take on the iterative process of culture design to create organizational culture *intentionally*?

- What personal *why* will keep you focused and motivated throughout the process of culture design?

Part One

Know What Matters

Chapter 1

Leaders Empathize

"Listening is not just hearing what someone tells you word for word. You have to listen with a heart. I don't want that to sound touchy-feely; it is not. It is very hard work."

—**Actress Anna Deavere Smith**

At the Chief Executives for Corporate Purpose (CECP) Summit in May 2024, James spoke on the final panel of the conference with Megan Myungwon Lee, CEO of Panasonic North America. When asked about cultivating empathy within her corporate culture, Lee said that she tried to consider how she would want her own children to be treated. We were struck by how well this mapped onto our own understanding of empathy—the greatest example of which is the empathy that a parent has for their child.

You may bristle at the idea, wanting a clear separation between colleagues, friends, and family. *It's just business*, you might think. *It's in no way the same as what I feel for relatives.* But that's not exactly true. We've all learned, especially since the pandemic, that life is not so neatly compartmentalized. The point is not that colleagues and family members are the same—they're not. The point is that your colleagues' humanity should be treated with the same empathy and respect as you'd give your child, parent, spouse, or sibling. They are no less human than those you love.

At that conference, themed "Purpose and Persistence," we heard from many people working in corporate sustainability, responsibility, giving, and other ESG and DEI-related fields. This purpose-driven work is central to the cultures that companies claim to embody (to be sure, it's not all the work that needs to be done with culture design, but it is core to it). In addition to their passion for the work, many people expressed a resounding frustration about the lack of buy-in on these topics from their CEOs and top leadership. These people heard Lee and found a yawning gap between her thoughtful, intentional approach and what they'd experienced in their organizations. We believe that gap exists because the daily practice of empathy is missing in most organizations, especially from and among leaders.

When you hear the word *empathy*, you might conflate that with some innate part of a leader's or person's character, but we don't see it that way. Empathy is a skill that can be practiced, and leaders who practice it are taking the first step to creating a culture by design.

Within the Culture Design framework, Leaders Empathize is your first step. It focuses on understanding, on a fundamental human level, what someone else—a worker, a customer, a community—is experiencing. These experiences all contribute to company culture, so you must understand them if you want to shape that culture.

Leaders who lack empathy aren't necessarily flawed or bad people. They're simply busy or haven't yet made the connection between practicing empathy and its positive effects on the culture and organization. But they can learn to incorporate it into their skill set.

A few of the skills leaders need to cultivate empathy are: Practice humility and curiosity, express vulnerability, and learn active listening. Let's look at each of these and how to practice them.

Practice Humility and Curiosity

Leaders like you have learned, through training and the natural position of authority, that you need to have all the answers. You're the ones who are making decisions, answering questions, and providing guidance. So it may take some practice to admit to yourself, "I'm not the expert here, and I need help to understand." Or "I haven't experienced what you have and need to learn from you." Or "Hey, I'm going to be straight up and tell my team what I'm working on to get this right." You may think you already know what areas you need to address in your culture, but you probably don't have a complete picture. Cultivating empathy requires leaders to leave assumptions and judgments at the door and to honor the fact that how they experience certain things—collaboration, work-life integration, overall career satisfaction, communication—isn't necessarily how their workers or customers experience them.

In processes that follow design thinking methodologies, the Leaders Empathize step is characterized by an open-mindedness on the part of the researchers or developers. When creating questions for interviews, they avoid leading questions and yes-or-no questions. As you ask others about their experiences, you too should avoid such propositions. Compare the kinds of answers you might get from these questions about something simple like the packaging for a new product:

- *Leading.* Do you like the simplicity and modern design of the packaging?

- *Yes-or-no.* Do you like the packaging?

- *Design thinking.* Talk to me about your feelings about the packaging.

The first question is not going to help you create the best packaging because you've already assigned it values *you* think it has (simple, modern). You're forcing the person you're talking to to take your point of view as a starting point. There's some curiosity here, but no humility.

The second question shows no curiosity; it's only meant to generate a data point, so you won't get much about the person's experience from their point of view. You will have no idea why they do or don't like the packaging.

The third prompt shows both humility and curiosity. It invites the person to talk about their feelings and is open-ended. This will give you the clearest picture of users' needs. (We always prefer open-ended questions.)

Now let's apply this to culture design by showing three examples of prompts leaders may use when talking to workers about organization-wide communications processes, noticing the humility and curiosity inherent in the third approach.

- *Leading.* What do you think of the lack of clarity in our communications?

- *Yes-or no.* Do you find our communications processes to be effective?

- *Culture design thinking.* What do you see as the strengths and challenges of our communications processes?

It should be noted that in both product design and culture design, you can (and should) have hypotheses about what people might think or feel or what their experiences may be like. But you must be curious and humble enough to admit the possibility that your hypothesis is wrong, that there are other possible explanations and important ideas.

When designing your organizational culture, you may hypothesize that a core problem is a lack of clear communications processes. But if your prompts are open-ended and you listen without prejudice, you may uncover issues that you hadn't even considered—that, say, the communications problem is a function of new tech tools your company has deployed.

It should be noted, and we'll cover this more below, that listening doesn't just happen in direct conversations. You can begin the process with indirect listening—finding culture clues in other forms of communication that happen in the organization through symbols, rituals, key processes, and celebrations.

Express Vulnerability

The leaders who flinched at the idea, noted above, that empathy at work is the same as empathy with family will likely struggle with vulnerability, too. But it's crucial to developing the empathy that will be the foundation of your culture design.

Vulnerability is related to, but different from, humility. Whereas humility is a belief about your *self*, your own openness to being wrong, not having answers, and learning, vulnerability is the expression of humility to *others*. Humility is a CEO choosing to listen to and learn from a frontline worker without assuming they know better than that worker. Vulnerability is saying to that frontline worker, "I don't understand, and I'd like you to bring me into your world."

Vulnerability is hard to embody for many in the workplace. We've been encouraged to shut off our emotions and grin and bear it. Leaders are trained to believe that they need to always appear strong, to have answers, and show unshakeable confidence, even if they don't feel it. Generally, however, this backfires, and the examples of leaders who do show vulnerability—we will hear from many—are often some of the most memorable and inspiring moments of culture design in businesses.

From James's Notepad

My friend Doug Conant, the former CEO of Campbell's Soup, would handwrite letters of gratitude and thanks to his teams. He's written over thirty thousand such notes. He's one of the most empathetic leaders we know. It has always reminded us that this work is about the long game, and that making even small gestures a habit can infuse intentional culture throughout the organization.

Without vulnerability, it will be hard to achieve empathy, because vulnerability invites connection; without it, others won't *really* talk with you. They won't feel comfortable sharing, and to develop empathy, people need to share. Opening up will build authenticity and trust.

To start expressing vulnerability, model the kind of conversations you'd like to have with people and for people to have with each other. This might look like sharing a time you overcame a hardship and how it affected how you look at leadership. James often shares the story of how his mom advocated for him when he was put in a remedial class in fifth grade, which taught him the importance of compassion, determination, and never taking no for an answer.

It could also mean sharing what's important to you within and beyond work. Maybe it's just a special ritual with your family, a passion for certain causes, or something as simple as Krista's love for musical theater. Sharing what matters most to you can help humanize you as a leader and member of the organization. If you can demonstrate that someone's full humanity is welcome in your workplace, you are more likely to have thoughtful and revealing conversations with your employees about their needs.

Learn Active Listening

Here we have one of the most underdeveloped, but also easy to sharpen, skills that will change your leadership in profound ways and, along with humility and vulnerability, fully unlocks the empathy you need to start intentionally designing culture.

Active listening just means that, when someone is speaking, you focus your energy on *only* what they are saying.

Listen. Really listen—and stop there. Your inclination might be to respond to everything you hear, or to start coming up with solutions even as you're listening. Do not do this. Do not assume you know what someone is going to say or what they might mean before they are done speaking. Do not interrupt. Do not try to solve. Do not even respond. Yet. Just make it a goal to understand others' experiences from their point of view. Just listen.

Most of the time, we don't practice active listening. It almost feels natural to want to jump in as soon as possible, to contribute to and build on the conversation. It's understandable that an intelligent and driven person like those of you reading this would want to share their great ideas as soon as possible or to signal what they feel or think as soon as possible: *Hey, I get you—here's something I can say to show you I'm empathetic.* And we've all experienced it, when we're talking to someone, and we can see their eyes move to some unmoored point past us. We can literally see them thinking about what to say instead of listening.

But not jumping ahead will benefit the growth of your empathy capabilities more. Learning to let your mental chatter take a back seat will help you hear what a person is saying better from their perspective—and with more nuance than if you fall into distracted patterns that come with hyper-connection. What do we miss when we're listening to respond, rather than to understand? How can we be more fully present with others? When you're able to switch your focus to understanding the other person, it opens you up to fully engage by listening more deeply and asking follow-up questions that could unlock a conversation that neither of you were expecting.

📱 From Krista's Notes App

As someone who has participated in several writing workshops, listening to absorb and understand has been invaluable to the way I write. As I take notes while being workshopped by others, and when I refrain from judgment while reading a classmate's work, I sharpen my skills as a critical reader and writer. It goes back to the classic aphorism, "Kill your darlings." The best writers—and leaders!—know how to put ego aside to best serve the work.

For example, as an executive, James routinely spent time with frontline workers to appreciate and understand their day-to-day challenges and opportunities, whether they were salespeople or restaurant workers or retail associates. Taking the time to truly hear people always had an impact on how he made the best decisions for all. And when Krista was conducting her initial user research for Kiki For The Future, her open-ended curiosity about her interviewees' lives, joys, and fears exposed her to a more intersectional perspective on sexuality and wellness, which has impacted the entire mission and tone of the brand and design of the app.

Archaeological Dig: The Culture Audit

You need the above skills to build empathy, but you will also combine them with background research to gain an understanding of your people and the current culture by surveying the signals you detect throughout the organization. We focused on those skills first because they're necessary to develop and use in your background research.

The sum of these parts—the background research and listening to your people—comprise what we call your Culture Audit, which we like to think of as an archaeological dig.

For the background research, you'll focus on these six tasks:

1. Review your written artifacts.

2. Explore and understand your rituals.

3. Understand your rewards.

4. Look for a say/do gap.

5. Excavate company symbols.

6. Review your HR processes.

Review your written artifacts

A great way to start taking stock of your culture is to *review your written artifacts*, including your mission, values, and purpose statements. You'll also want to gain a clear understanding of the roots and history behind these statements. How did you get to where you are now? Do you feel like your mission statement and written values align to how your people show up every day? Leaders with a clear understanding of these fundamental documents and histories can use them as guideposts as they build culture; or they can work to change them to better represent the culture they want to intentionally design (more on this to come).

Brenna Davis, CEO of the nation's largest organic produce wholesaler, Organically Grown Company (OGC), emphasizes the importance of honoring the company's roots. She has a reverence for the founders and retired alumni of the company, who at OGC are referred to as "elders." Davis told us about how the company has upheld its founders' mission by establishing the first perpetual purpose trust in the country. Founded in 1978 by a group of farmers, OGC has long centered its work on its mission: to promote and inspire the growth of the organic agriculture movement. In 2018, it took that history into account when it restructured to transfer ownership to the Sustainable Food and Agriculture Perpetual Purpose Trust.[1] This allows OGC to focus on its long-term purpose instead of short-term shareholder returns. With this act, purpose and culture became inextricably linked and inextricably tied to how the business runs. Now, the organization's relationship to its purpose affects how work gets done, how meetings are run, and how decisions get made. It is by understanding its history that OGC was able to carve out a path for its long-term future.

For you, revisiting your company's mission, purpose, values, and history may spark some initial ideas about where there may be gaps between your purported culture and how it shows up. When you compare your mission statement or documented values to organizational policies and tactics, do they match? You may find that you've strayed too far from your original purpose and that you need to find a way back.

History can also reveal how far you've come. For legacy companies, there will often be lessons of what not to do and clues as to how to reconcile past wrongs with your vision for the future. Whether it is ties to systems of oppression or dishonest business practices, history is not to be forgotten or swept under the rug, but to be learned from. Follow those hunches to the next part of your dig and document them as you design questions for surveys, interviews, or roundtables that you may conduct later. Keep your personal notes handy in a spreadsheet, Google Doc, or—if you're like James—a good old-fashioned legal pad. The most important thing is keeping track of the work you're doing here in a way that will be most accessible to you and your team when it's time to go out and talk and listen to your stakeholders.

Explore and understand your rituals

Next, *explore rituals*. From the way you start and end meetings to how you celebrate employee contributions to your annual company retreat, rituals are the day-to-day traditions that reinforce your culture. At meetings, people have used everything from a routine check-in to see how their team members are feeling to a moment of gratitude shared at the onset of meetings.

At the Honest Company (where James is board chair), CEO Carla Vernón aims to create psychological safety and creativity, so at town halls she asks employees to share which of a preselected set of Pixar characters represents what mood or energy they're embodying in the moment. (The options include the characters of Joy or Fear from *Inside Out*, or the relaxed optimism of Crush the Turtle in *Finding Nemo*.) And to foster a culture of open communication, Lee Wallace, CEO of fair trade coffee producer Peace Coffee, has instituted an agenda item in every meeting that asks what needs to be communicated and to whom as a result of the meeting.[2] Keeping everyone on the same page with the information they need to succeed is a key part of her change management agenda as she grows the company. Simple activities repeated over and over have a cumulative effect on culture.

Many of you may be thinking, *That kind of stuff is not for me*—you don't see a connection between results and asking people how they feel at every meeting. We know it works and encourage you to be vulnerable and get out of your comfort zone and try it. But also recognize that not all rituals are about feelings. Other types of rituals that reinforce culture are brief weekly check-ins about the successes and challenges of the week, a daily review of a tenet of centering customer needs at staff meetings, or a biweekly cross-functional review and prioritization of issues that have come up during those two weeks.

Celebratory rituals often take the form of a company picnic or holiday party, but consider what it would mean to create a ritual that was uniquely suited to your company and colleagues. OGC has long celebrated its annual tomato war, where team members go out at the end of tomato season and throw overripe tomatoes at each other.[3] When we heard about this, we immediately wanted an invite to the event, and it struck us that most companies don't have celebrations with quite so much personality and distinction. The fact that OGC does signals to us that that culture is being intentionally designed. Do you have any traditions that are uniquely suited to your culture? Do you have any ideas for new traditions you could institute? This is the intentionality piece of building culture through rituals. None of the examples we give you here will be appropriate to you, but they should show you how specific and apt to the culture your rituals can be.

Understand your rewards

In addition to rituals, you should *understand your rewards*. Rewards and rituals are closely related. They can impact your employees' experience of your culture, for better and for worse. While rituals are activities that happen independent of performance (you can have a tomato fight any time), rewards are what you do to recognize positive behavior that maps to the culture you want to instill. They may be formal or informal.

As you explore the rewards your organization offers, also pay close attention to what you *don't* acknowledge or reward. For instance, have you ever rewarded or recognized workers who took all their vacation? Imagine what that would signal about your culture. Rewarding only those who come in early and stay late disregards the fullness of one's humanity (including parenthood, disability status, and mental well-being). Taking only hard skills into consideration for promotions tells employees that soft skills like compassion, communication, and conflict-resolution are not valued.

It's important to note that no leader is purposely attempting to reward bad behavior or negative cultural traits. They are well-intentioned: Doesn't working long hours make you a hard worker? (Though research suggests a weak correlation at best.[4]) Our critique of such a reward system doesn't come from a desire to punish those who put in long hours or who have carefully honed their hard skills. We are suggesting that we reframe the very definition of what it means to be a good worker. Does a good worker have to embody just those kinds of attributes? Or could a good worker simply be someone who completes high-quality work in a timely fashion and is pleasant to be around? You get to decide the criteria that best aligns with your desired culture—and create rewards to match.

Look for a say/do gap

The other side of the rewards coin is discipline, and part of your dig should be to look at how unwanted behavior is addressed and look for a *say/do gap*. If you claim to have a zero tolerance for certain behaviors but time and again have let them go, your employees learn that those behaviors are acceptable, and they learn that yours is a culture of "say one thing, do another"—a bad place to be. Are there gaps between people, with some allowed to behave a certain way while others are not? Is there a lack of accountability, poor communication, or low engagement or bad habits that are tolerated or ignored? This kind of inconsistency becomes its own informal, harmful reward system. Conversely, you should also look at whether the things you have been correcting have been addressed with your core values in mind. Are workplace issues dealt with empathetically? Are the same consequences doled out regardless of who the person is? Is there a system in place for how to deal with bad behavior, and is it followed in practice? How swiftly are issues addressed?

Excavate company symbols

The next part of your archaeological dig may feel more existential: *excavate your company symbols.*

Have you ever thought about what your logo means? Why your company uses certain colors? You may not think visual cues relate much to company culture, but if they didn't affect our psychology, companies wouldn't spend millions of dollars on branding. Your brand identity is more than an external marketing tool—it also affects how your employees (and customers) perceive your company. At the Honest Company, Carla Vernón is proud to espouse the butterfly symbol in the company's logo. For her, it is directly connected to the company's culture and purpose. She describes how the quiet strength of the pollinating insect has become a metaphor for their brand promise internally and for consumers. Symbols can reveal subtle underpinnings of how culture has been showing up for years, maybe even since your company was founded—

like the way Vernón calls her team members "butterfly fam" or how people may react to Slack messages with a butterfly emoji—that reinforce a sense of team camaraderie in the organization.

An organization's physical space is another symbol and one that you have so much control over to intentionally design. An office wall lined with photographs of executives is a symbol that employees will see differently than a wall lined with pictures of frontline workers on the job or customers celebrating your products. An open-concept office may tell employees that their workplace is collaborative. Features like gender-neutral bathrooms and accessible offices let everyone know that a company fosters inclusion. Conversely, a workplace with lots of stairs and no ramps or elevators may convey a message that some people are an afterthought. How are people spread through the space? Are they siloed by department or do people from different departments intermingle in spaces? Do executives work in a separate space, or have larger, more closed-off spaces?

We're not espousing any one approach to office design; we're saying that the choices you make contribute to the culture. So not being intentional about space means you are letting your culture happen rather than designing it yourself. Match how you use your office design to how you want your culture to be. Separate space for executives may be fine for hierarchical culture. If you desire a culture of innovation, research shows that "collisions" between people—especially people from different disciplines and backgrounds and organizational levels—are one of the best things you can create, so design your space to encourage such interactions.[5] The thing you can't do is just assume culture will overcome the design of your physical space.

Symbols like style guides, logos, and brand standards are also all useful tools for internal culture in addition to their obvious external marketing value. Especially for those working remotely, these elements, in addition to artifacts like the mission and vision statements, are the primary way employees interact with their company's culture. A style guide, for example, can convey your company's values: the language and imagery you consistently use in your internal communications influences the way your employees think and get work done. Adding simple guidelines like "we capitalize the 'B' in 'Black'" or "use captions and transcripts for audio and video communications whenever possible" can shift the language and eventually the mental frameworks of the people in your company. One way to make style guides more inclusive is to look at the media guides put out by organizations such as GLAAD.[6]

The images and videos used in your branding matter as well. From the diversity of stock photos and illustrations to the subtleties of your logo, ensure that your marketing collateral squares with the culture you would like to build. Think of Duolingo, the language-learning app that regularly goes viral for its quirky, meme-centric TikToks, a mirror of the scrappy and playful startup energy it's worked to cultivate in its offices. Or take Patagonia, which doubles down on its commitment to the planet and work-life integration through its anti–Black Friday marketing campaigns.[7]

Review your HR processes

Finally, as you conclude your dig, *review HR processes*. What are the steps involved in hiring, onboarding, reviews, promotions, firing, and offboarding? How do you create your job posts? Where do you recruit from? What do the formal and informal succession planning processes look like? Enlist the help of your HR leaders and managers to get a comprehensive look at their various processes and procedures.

This can help you identify where your stated commitments aren't matching up with what is happening in practice. For example, you may say you are committed to gender parity in your workplace, but are your HR policies supportive of mothers? See table 1-1 for the essential processes to examine and some questions to consider.

TABLE 1-1

Essential HR processes to consider

Process	Questions
Recruitment, hiring, and onboarding	Where are you recruiting from?
	How do you write job descriptions?
	How are interview questions created?
Benefits	Are the available benefits the same for all genders (e.g., parental leave, partner benefits)?
	How do benefits align with industry standards?
	Do you encourage people to use their benefits (e.g., vacation time)?
Training	What training is available for new employees? How long is orientation?
	What about upskilling opportunities for seasoned employees?
Reviews	How do you mitigate bias in reviews?
Promotions and succession planning	How are promotions determined?
Employee relations	What are the formal processes for complaints?
	How permissive of misconduct is your company?
Firing	How often are people fired?
Offboarding	What is the employee turnover rate?
	What is the exit interview process like?
	Do you conduct stay interviews?

In addition to the companywide people systems and processes put in place by HR, leaders should also take a close look at how other departments function. This can be as straightforward as "How often do people get paid?" and as complex as "How do we decide when to launch new products?" Some other examples of the things to look at here include:

- How do different departments communicate internally and interdepartmentally?

- Where do you use automation in your procedures?

- How do IT issues get resolved?

For every case above, write down the answers to the questions, map them to the culture you want to create, and see if there are obvious gaps. For example, if you want to build a strong culture of work-life balance for your employees, but your answers indicate that you offer only minimum required parental leave and do not have mechanisms to ensure that people are using their vacation, then you are not building your culture intentionally. Those are places to make changes.

Putting Your Findings to Work

All of this may feel overwhelming, especially if you are a leader at a large corporation with many disparate systems and processes. Even leaders at smaller companies may be surprised by just how many systems they have at their organizations. This is why we use the metaphor of an archaeological dig: It's hard, painstaking work. Sometimes it's slow. It's detail-oriented and requires patience and practice. You will come up with volumes of documentation during your dig.

FIGURE 1-1

Mapping your archaeological dig

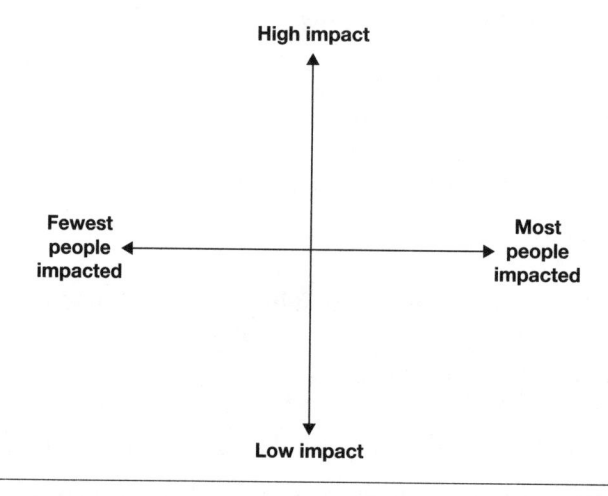

```
                        High impact
                             ▲
                             │
    Fewest                   │                    Most
    people   ◄────────────────────────────►      people
   impacted                  │                  impacted
                             │
                             ▼
                        Low impact
```

So what can you do to make it manageable?

We suggest mapping it. When prioritizing which systems, processes, and activities to look at closely, you may want to visualize by using a matrix like the one shown in figure 1-1. This can help you pinpoint where to focus your precious resources. The top-right quadrant is your sweet spot for culture transformation through design.

Figure 1-2 offers an example of a matrix that was filled out during an archaeological dig for one of our clients, a two-hundred-employee tech company. The challenge for this company, which was made up of a distributed team including R&D, sales, and manufacturing units, was to build a high-performance culture that would be sustainable as the company continued to scale rapidly. Due to the complexity and size of the R&D team, investing in leadership training for that business unit ended up being a high-impact focus in addition to executive

FIGURE 1-2

A mapped archaeological dig

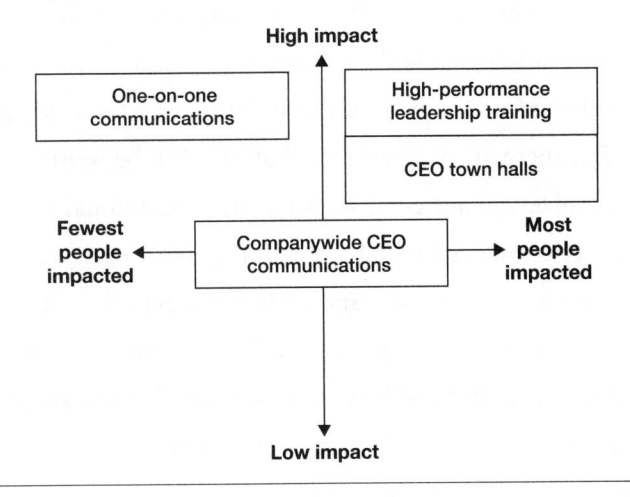

```
                         High impact
                             ▲
   ┌─────────────────┐       │   ┌─────────────────────┐
   │   One-on-one    │       │   │  High-performance   │
   │  communications │       │   │  leadership training│
   └─────────────────┘       │   ├─────────────────────┤
                             │   │   CEO town halls    │
                             │   └─────────────────────┘
  Fewest          ┌──────────────────────┐         Most
  people     ◄────│   Companywide CEO    │────►    people
  impacted        │    communications    │         impacted
                  └──────────────────────┘
                             │
                             ▼
                         Low impact
```

team training. The colocated manufacturing team was already high-performing, and uniting culture functions like quarterly town halls, an annual company summit, and monthly extended leadership sessions were identified as helpful but with a secondary impact. CEO communications affect the entire company but are most effective in concert with higher-priority actions. Although one-on-one communication can provide useful insight, it was identified as a lower priority as this company was focused on growth, systems, and sustainability.

Like this company, you likely won't have elements that fit squarely into each quadrant, but the visual approximation is a quick way to get your mind around how to prioritize. After you identify the high-impact areas that affect the largest number of people, you can dig deeper into the above areas. Here are a set of steps for unveiling these systems that you can follow and tweak to your needs.

Look at internally available documentation

Many of your systems, especially within HR, will be available in internal documentation. These documents are a great place to start and will provide you with a basic understanding of what is supposed to happen. But there are also systems that may not be written down or easily accessible on your company's intranet. Additionally, what happens in practice may not match up with the stated procedures. Sometimes this is for a good reason, and understanding why folks are doing what they are is as important as the what and the how. This is why you'll need to engage directly with department leaders and administrators through surveys and interviews, always positioned as open-ended, always using active listening.

Send out departmental surveys

The goal of these surveys is to understand how work really gets done. These should be filled out both by department heads and by administrators, at the very least. Administrators are often the most familiar with the nitty-gritty of how systems work at any organization. They're the ones handling scheduling, emails, planning events, submitting reports, and so forth. These surveys should be designed with a combination of open-ended and yes-or-no, rating-based questions. You want to understand both what people are doing in practice and whether it is working. Keep all questions, including open-ended questions, specific. Instead of asking "What kind of systems do you use in your typical workday?" you might ask "Which systems (mandated or of your own creation) do you use to help you with completing administrative tasks?" The limitation of the survey is that the questions still need to be broad enough to apply to everyone, unless you create different surveys for different job functions, which would be tedious and time-consuming. A better option would be to buffer this with interviews with select members of each department.

Conduct interviews with managers and team members

These interviews will give you an additional opportunity to get a full understanding of the way systems play out in practice. You can conduct them simultaneously with the survey or after you've received survey results. The former may be more efficient, but the benefit of the latter is the ability to design your interviews with follow-up questions to the survey. In either scenario, tailoring interview questions to different departments and job functions will allow you to get the most comprehensive point of view on the systems at play throughout the organization. Remember to practice humility, vulnerability, and active listening in the interviews.

Roundtables, town halls, and one-on-ones

When creating formal opportunities for conversation with your employees, you'll want to choose the format based on your company size, industry, and the focus of your work. Smaller groups give you the opportunity to dig into the nitty-gritty but may not always be feasible, and in a large company will only offer a small segment of experiences. Events like town halls and listening sessions, on the other hand, give you the option to touch a broader population. Whatever you choose, there are options to infuse the principles of empathetic listening in creative ways. Early in his tenure at Jamba Juice, James held a town hall where he had people write on index cards what they hoped he would change and what they hoped would remain the same. This was a way for him to meaningfully connect with the heart of the organization, describe what he valued as he joined the company, and understand how he could best lead his teams to reach the success he knew was possible.

You can also use these conversations as an opportunity to express your overall vision for the organization while emphasizing that you are open to feedback. In this case, you'll want to have a clear mechanism for employee input, be it a specific email inbox or a Slack channel, where you can easily compile and react to feedback where appropriate.

Distill your findings

Once you've finished your audit of current documentation, completed a round of surveys, and conducted departmental interviews, you will need to summarize and present your findings to the team working on your cultural transformation. Use automation tools to your advantage here—they can help you more efficiently identify trends and patterns in your interviews and survey responses. Larger organizations can consider subjecting the massive volume of feedback to sentiment analysis tools as well. After identifying the systems at play in key impact areas, you're ready to continue your archaeological expedition.

. . .

The focus of this first Leaders Empathize step is for leaders to build empathy for their workforce as a means to an end—to get the most out of the archaeological dig. But we'd be remiss if we didn't talk about the ways that empathy can be an end in and of itself, something that's integrated into the cultural fabric you're designing for the organization. It shouldn't just be a tool deployed to see where you're at, it should be part of the culture itself. It's no accident that UX design firms are built as inherently empathetic cultures.

Empathy allows you to shift, shape, and transform culture if it's built into the way you do business at every level. Communication and conversation are key levers when it comes to building empathy. Dave Peacock, CEO of Advantage Solutions, a seventy-thousand-person services company working at the intersection of retail and consumer products, has always been a leader who inspired us. Peacock's breadth of experience as a senior leader across many industries has given him a unique vantage point on building intentional cultures that always put people first. When he began his tenure at Advantage in 2023, he knew he had to start by hiring critical employees, his new chief communications officer and CHRO, Kelli Hammersmith and Pamela Morris-Thornton, respectively. He restructured these positions so that they both report to him, as communications and people-centric roles are so critical. He told us, "I find that 95 percent, maybe more, of issues that exist, whether it be in a company, in a family, in society more broadly, are a communication problem."[8] With comms officer Hammersmith, he was able to build a smoother and more transparent flow of communication into the company. The continuous two-way exchange of information allows for helpful feedback and course-correction—it is an intentional choice to shape the culture as one of open conversation. CEO Peacock has also recently instituted Moments That Matter, a series of conversations that deal with personal challenges that his workforce has faced, such as raising children in a blended marriage. These conversations are meant to help people connect on a human level, finding threads of commonality among all their differences. In this divided climate, it has become more urgent than ever to find points of connection that remind us of our mutual humanity.

Another example of driving empathy throughout an organization comes from a national retailer we've worked with, which developed a storytelling series. These enterprise-wide sessions comprise five- to ten-minute speeches from two to four associates, typically focusing on a theme like "Widening Your Mindset." The conversations are meant to provide a forum for employees at all levels to share their different stories to help build a more inclusive culture. The goals of the series are to amplify and celebrate diverse lived experiences while modeling empathy (through vulnerability, humility, and active listening), develop the core competency of authenticity, and to create spaces for psychological safety.

When setting forth on developing empathy as your first step in intentional culture design, don't forget about the relationship with clients, members, or customers—relationships that are often overlooked in this process. Are the people you serve at the forefront of your decision-making? Tony Wells, the longtime marketing executive and Marines veteran, found his time at USAA unique among his decades working at more than ten different companies. A leader who has long been in the business of people and communications, he told us that during his tenure as chief brand officer he was struck by how central the company's members were to the way it did business. Every meeting was started with a "mission moment," connecting the meeting agenda and intended outcomes to USAA's mission—ensuring the financial security of its members and the entire military community. The organization also had Zero Day PT, a voluntary annual tradition that aims to build empathy for its members. Employees are picked up at 4 a.m. and bused out to a field, where they get a taste of what military boot camp is like. Additionally, on Member Services Day, the company leaders spent a day observing their member services call center reps to develop an understanding of both the needs of the members and the challenges faced by their frontline workers. All-hands-on-deck rituals like these made USAA's culture stand out for Wells as a company that paid special attention to integrating its values at every level.[9]

Empathy is not just a feeling, but an intentional, daily practice. It takes consistency, humility, vulnerability, active listening, patience, and a genuine care and curiosity for others. Whether you are finding ways to practice it yourself or are modeling and integrating empathy for your entire organization, what matters is not perfection, but dedication.

Takeaways

- Empathy is the bedrock of designing culture.
- Cultivating empathy requires listening with attention and curiosity.
- The Leaders Empathize step in the Culture Design framework means to fully understand the current cultural context.
- People systems and practices are key signifiers of culture.
- Empathy can be integrated throughout a culture through ritual and communication.

Chapter 2

Leaders Define the Reality

"The culture you have in your organization is the sum of all the wanted behaviors that you celebrate minus all the unwanted behaviors that you tolerate."

—Shake Shack founder Danny Meyer

Your culture audit may—actually, it's likely to—reveal gaps and pain points that you never would have considered. That's the power of empathy—it helps us overcome being blinded by our own vantage points, which is why it's so key to seek out multiple perspectives. Krista experienced this through her design thinking process while building her app. The version of the Empathize process she did with potential app users exposed her own blind spots. Going in, she was confident she knew the pain points in sexual health for the LGBTQIA+ community. But through her audit she discovered a real need for medically accurate, queer-inclusive sex education, which she hadn't considered. In creating her app and website, Kiki For The Future, Krista aimed to fill that inclusion gap while creating medically accurate, easy-to-read content that could be useful for *all*.

Without actually doing the empathy work, she never would have come up with the idea at all. But since she did, she could redefine her effort to build a culture around the app. You're going to be doing the same thing, regardless of the kind of organization you're intentionally designing culture for. You did the audit, the archaeological dig. Now you can compare what you found to the hypothesis you had about the culture and define the culture you want to create clearly and fully.

For Advantage Solutions CEO Dave Peacock, empathy is what has allowed him to consider both "the singular and the plural." It allows him to take an integrative approach to decision-making in his people-first leadership style. In his seventy-thousand-person business, considering both the individual and the seventy thousand means making difficult and strategic layoff decisions for the greater good while also treating each person with dignity and respect by reconsidering their severance policies.[1]

If you haven't gotten out the sticky notes and whiteboards yet, this is a great time to do so.

From James's Notepad

Even for those of you who are Google Docs lovers like Krista (I've never been a big fan), this is one time I recommend listening to your elders, getting your eyes off the screen and getting out scratch paper and your favorite writing utensil. Normally, I'd say use what tool you are comfortable with, but I firmly believe that at this point in the process, the tactile experiences of writing, sticking, and reviewing paper notes really unlocks another side of your brain.

There are several tools that James uses with clients (and has used throughout his career) that help bring definition to a problem, identify key areas to focus on, and tackle an action plan to build the culture. This is the Leaders Define the Reality step of the Culture Design framework, when you will zero in the actions that matter to your organization to create the blueprint for your intentional culture design efforts. It's the second part of knowing what matters, and it will help you bring clarity to your cultural context.

During his time as CEO of Jamba Juice, James used many of the following tools and frameworks with his team in their turnaround efforts when he was defining the culture he wanted to create. These tools allowed them to create a clear assessment of where the reality of the culture stood and how it needed to shift to enable their strategic goals. We are sharing the tools and frameworks that follow to give you a breadth of options that may work for your organization, and we include examples of how James applied them at Jamba Juice as well as inspiration from other leaders. Use one, use them all, flex and remix them to your needs. We see this as less of a how-to guide and more of a toolkit that can be customized to your own culture, industry, and vision.

STAR Method

A fundamental prioritization tool James has used throughout his career is the strategic thinking and results (STAR) method, originated

FIGURE 2-1

The STAR method

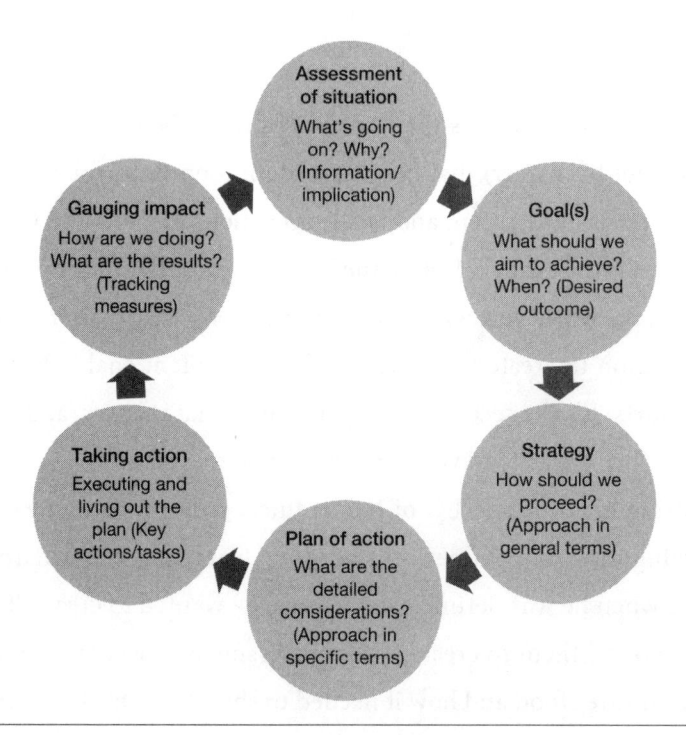

- **Assessment of situation**: What's going on? Why? (Information/implication)
- **Goal(s)**: What should we aim to achieve? When? (Desired outcome)
- **Strategy**: How should we proceed? (Approach in general terms)
- **Plan of action**: What are the detailed considerations? (Approach in specific terms)
- **Taking action**: Executing and living out the plan (Key actions/tasks)
- **Gauging impact**: How are we doing? What are the results? (Tracking measures)

by organizational theorist Jay R. Galbraith in the 1960s.[2] This approach is broken into six steps, seen in figure 2-1. The first four steps: assessment of situation, goal(s), strategy, and plan of action, will be most relevant to Leaders in the Define the Reality step.

At each of these steps, there are questions to consider, shown in table 2-1.

To give you an example of how this plays out in real situations, we share a high-level overview of James's use of the STAR method at Jamba Juice in table 2-2.

With the charge of "save the company," James's team at Jamba Juice knew they needed to be more focused on building a high-performance

TABLE 2-1

The STAR method: Questions to consider

STAR step	Questions and goals
Assessment of situation. You will have already begun this part of the STAR method in the Leaders Empathize step of the Culture Design process.	What are our strengths and weaknesses in this situation? What are our opportunities? What are our threats? What are our sources of competitive advantage? What are the cause-and-effect factors governing the situation? What is the outlook for desired outcomes/profit?
Goal(s). Define a specific, measurable, time-bound goal or set of goals for your culture transformation.	What can realistically be achieved in this situation? To what extent is the goal contingent or dependent on the key cause-and-effect factors? What is the time frame?
Strategy. Consider a variety of potential creative strategies to achieve your goal or goals.	Consider at least three alternative strategies. Challenge yourself to be creative. Learn from your competitors. Use cause-and-effect factors as the core of your strategies. Identify and use sources of competitive advantage, including time and timing. Consider cause and ease of execution. Select the most effective overall strategy (will often be a composite). If strategy fails, what are our contingencies?
Plan of action. Settle on an action plan following deliberate parameters.	For each action step, define what, who, when, and required resources, including financial estimates. Ensure that action steps are consistent with the selected strategy and work from or on the key cause-and-effect factors.

(continued)

TABLE 2-1 *(continued)*

The STAR method: Questions to consider

STAR step	Questions and goals
Taking action. Execute the plan.	Communicate fully.
	Ensure disciplined implementation.
	Remain flexible, seek feedback, adjust efforts.
	Deploy contingencies when/if needed.
Gauging impact: Measure results.	Identify key measures in advance.
	Add measures as experience dictates.
	Tracking progress on milestones is only part of what is important.
	Monitor financial impact and people impact.
	Regularly check for changes in the situation.

culture that was collaborative, more cross-functional, and more diverse at every level. To define what mattered most, James combined cross-functional action-learning teams with the STAR model work to enable the future by shifting the culture. Action-learning teams, which may also be called sprint teams or task forces, are small, cross-functional groups designed to help organizations innovate and find creative solutions to sticky problems. These groups start with a team of fifteen to twenty people, with breakout groups of five to eight. At Jamba Juice, James used these teams to study growth initiatives like international expansion, rapid menu changes, and opening more stores in airports. He found that these teams made change smoother and more efficient.

Middle managers should always be a part of every action-learning team because of their pivotal role in cascading—or stalling—change

TABLE 2-2

James's use of the STAR method at Jamba Juice

STAR steps	Examples from Jamba Juice
Assessment of situation. You will have already begun this part of the STAR method in the Leaders Empathize step of the Culture Design process.	James took over in 2008 as CEO. Company needed significant turnaround. Cash runway was running out. Same-store sales were faltering. Company needed cultural shift to become high-performance and results-oriented.
Goal(s). Define a specific, measurable, time-bound goal or set of goals for your culture transformation.	Reengage culture with key stakeholders. Significantly increase sales. Improve customer service.
Strategy. Consider a variety of potential creative strategies to achieve your goal or goals.	Introduce a multipronged strategic plan that uses transforming the culture as a critical foundation.
Plan of action. Settle on an action plan following deliberate parameters.	Underpin every action with culture transformation. Invest in product innovation; for example, steel-cut oatmeal and healthier beverages. Deploy additional tools and training to support restaurants.
Taking action. Execute the plan.	Detail tactical plans for each action item.
Gauging impact. Measure the results.	Conduct culture engagement surveys. Perform weekly, quarterly, annual review of same-store sales and customer satisfaction.

in an organization. You can also jump-start the culture you're designing with intentionality around the people you select for these teams. You should deliberately design the teams using the values of your defined culture as guidance. You may want to underscore inclusion by building diverse teams or include people who exemplify traits or skills you would like to emphasize, especially if those people have previously been overlooked. This can send a signal that you are committed to change and will also make the team more likely to bear solutions and learnings that are in line with your vision for the future.

Future-Back Method

One thing you might realize once you've begun to define the reality of your current and desired culture is just how much work you have to do—all while operating a business. Your culture audit will uncover many gaps and areas to change, but you can only focus on a few at a time. You'll need to prioritize.

A great complementary filtering tool to help you prioritize is the *future-back* method, which is a way to envision the end point you'd like to reach and then work your way back from that future to see what you need to do to get there. Though there are numerous step-by-step methods of using future-back thinking, James found it most useful as a mindset. In the case of culture design, you are defining the ideal culture needed to achieve your forward-thinking goals.

What will be required for your future vision to be possible? This mental framework will help you determine both the what and the how your organization will focus on to achieve the next levels of growth. The future-back concept is one James has used as an operator, first at Nestlé Purina, then at Gillette, Safeway, and Jamba Juice. The goal was always to clearly define what strategies would advantage the company, department, or function. Whether you think of it as a foundation, pillar, or enabler, *culture always ties back to strategy*.

An archetypal example of future-back thinking is Netflix. Down to the name of the company, the streaming giant's founders were looking ahead to what would be possible in the future, rather than relying on current technology capabilities. They invested in online movies along with their flagship (now-defunct) DVD-by-mail business, their vision of leading the way in streaming technology aligning with their strategic priorities to reach millions of subscribers with their movies and series. We don't have to tell you how that turned out.

To execute on this kind of visionary, forward-thinking strategy, a company like Netflix needs to have a culture that cultivates innovation, collaboration, and a fearlessness around risk—something that would become clear by working from the future back. Likewise, creating your vision will enable you to work backward and define the kind of culture required for success. Depending on your industry, you will typically want to pick a time five to ten years from now. It should be far enough away to stretch your mindset, but not so far in the future that it becomes too abstract.

The future-back method is a great tool for bringing definition to culture design because it brings the actionable strategic details together with big moonshot goals. This has the benefit of making these visions feel more tangible for the stakeholders you need onboard. Once you understand where the gaps and opportunities are, you can begin to construct your vision for the future. Think about where you can grow your current capabilities, where you can find new opportunities in your current business model, and where there are new horizons to explore. Then the crucial step for your purpose is to ask, *What kind of culture do I need to build to reach those goals?* What actions, habits, rituals, and beliefs will be necessary to achieve your vision?

Even before embarking on his turnaround of Jamba Juice, James was already a future-back thinker who knew the value of dreaming big. His vision—of Jamba as a leading healthy lifestyle brand with strong financial growth—didn't align with the current state. Friends saw a flagging company, with a limited menu that hadn't adapted to seasonality, in the middle of a financial crisis, and said "James, why would you take that job?" But it was his future-back mindset that allowed him to design an innovative, cross-functional culture and achieve his long-term vision. Culture design, bolstered by future-back thinking, requires leaders who are in it for the long haul.

At Jamba Juice, James and his team also used creative, out-of-the-box techniques to carefully hone their desired future state. This included receiving collective input from the leadership team to create an illustrated plan, which they compiled into a booklet. It was a literal blueprint, a physical manifestation of the Leaders Define the Reality step in culture design. Creative tools like hiring a live sketch or graphic recording artist (or enlisting an artistic member of your team) can help unlock your thinking. For Jamba Juice, this groundwork opened the possibility for a culture of creativity, innovation, and cross-functional and cross-level collaboration. As the team was encouraged to dream big and began working together more effectively, they were able to create and execute against James's iterative turnaround plan. The first part, called Blend 1.0, included reducing costs, reinvigorating the franchise system, expanding the menu, and leveraging consumer packaged goods (CPG) licensing. The next part, Blend 2.0: Strategic Turnaround, continued to refine Jamba's CPG strategy, began international expansion, and launched JambaGo, smaller format self-serve smoothie stations. By the end of 2012, Jamba

Juice broke even and turned a profit for the first time in six years. The realization of this long-term vision wouldn't have been possible without intentional culture design, and the culture design was likewise shaped by the strategy. They work in lockstep.

At its core, a culture transformation is also a transformation of your business. Designing your culture means designing your future business outcomes. To convert your vision into a strategy, decide on three to four areas to invest in and walk back your milestones from there in two- to three-year increments, as with the iterative Blend plans at Jamba.

Write the Press Release First

The future-back method is not dissimilar to Amazon's press release method for product development, which James has also used with his teams. With this approach, product teams begin by writing a mock press release announcing the future product to the target customer. This helps them center who they are creating for throughout the product development process. It is also a quick gut check for the product's viability. At Amazon, these press releases typically include: the product's name; the intended customer; the problem the product solves; the benefits to the customer; a quote from someone at the company explaining in an inspirational way why they developed the product and what they hope it will do for your customer; a call to action telling the customer how to take advantage of the product right away; and an optional FAQ answering the business or tactical questions about building the product.[3]

From Krista's Notes App

Without realizing it, I've always thought like this for everything from personal milestones to big career dreams to plotting novels. When I'm starting a new creative project, it helps me to write the synopsis first and work backward from the end product (a bestseller, naturally) to create a detailed outline and eventually start in on the writing. Looking back at the synopsis keeps me focused on the big (major motion) picture when I'm in the weeds trying to get my main character to do what I want. I suspect many of us do this, or parts of this, without realizing it, so once you set out on doing it with your culture, it may feel familiar. By being just a little more intentional about working future-back, you will be building your culture more effectively.

To apply this method to your culture design, you might retool this outline to look something like:

- *The product's name.* Is there a word, set of words, or a phrase that describes your vision for your culture?

- *The intended customer.* The employees, suppliers, clients, and other stakeholders affected by your culture plan.

- *The problem the product solves.* What gaps have you identified in your culture?

- *The benefits to the customer.* How will your workplace and business outcomes improve?

- *A quote from someone at the company explaining in an inspirational way why you developed the product and what you hope it will do for your customer.* Consider including a statement from your CEO outlining why this transformation is important.

- *A call to action telling the customer how to take advantage of the product right away.* What can your employees do today to take part in the transformation?

- *Optional: FAQ answering the business or tactical questions about building the product.* What doubts or questions can you foresee?

Table 2-3 shows an example of how Krista may have created the press release first when she was envisioning the culture for Kiki For The Future's team. Krista would use the finished product to collaborate with her team to cocreate culture. As a small startup, Kiki For The Future had the advantage of building culture by design from the get-go. The press release format has the added benefit of being a jumping-off point for future iterations of your message. It is used as an exercise, but the initial document you create may end up being part of your communications strategy.

After creating the press release, the next steps that Amazon takes are evaluating the opportunity, discovering solutions and getting stakeholder approval, and creating the backlog and assigning tasks. These steps will look the same in your culture design process, which after defining the reality and creating your action plan will follow the progression of implementation, iteration, and bringing culture to life with stakeholder buy-in.

TABLE 2-3

Krista's press release

Culture design "press release" elements	Kiki For The Future examples
Product's name	Inclusive, fun, collaborative
Intended customer	Team members and ultimately users and subscribers
Problem the product solves	Clear workflow systems and training processes that will allow the culture to remain healthy at scale
Benefits to the customer	Increased efficiency, reach a wider audience with our vital education, grow a close-knit community during a difficult time
Quote from someone at the company explaining in an inspirational way why you developed the product and what you hope it will do for your customer	"Centering queer health, wellness, and joy is more important than ever. We aim to cut through the noise to provide approachable, medically accurate, and easily digestible sexual health resources for the LGBTQIA+ community."
Call to action telling the customer how to take advantage of the product right away	"I want to hear your voice! I will make an effort to ask you for feedback regularly, and I encourage you to reach out whenever you have questions or ideas."
Optional: FAQs answering business or tactical questions about building the product	FAQ: How will I prioritize the health of the culture? *By empowering my team members with both the tools and guidance they need* as well as the *decision-making power necessary to work effectively.* FAQ: Is it possible to have an organizational culture on a small team? *Yes! Put a few people together and a dynamic will emerge whether you design it or not.*

Additional Tools

In addition to these pen-and-paper methods of bringing definition to the reality of your culture, you can also use technology. Could you use

AI to pull out major themes from interview transcripts? Use data visualization to get a clearer picture of your survey results? You're already using tools like these to increase efficiency in other parts of your business, so there's no reason you shouldn't bring them into your culture design process.

You can also borrow from the world of tech design and create a culture problem statement. Using the general template "[User/stakeholder] needs [stakeholder need] because [insight/current gap]" as a guideline, think of this of an elevator pitch of your cultural ambition. This can help you communicate your plans throughout your organization. An example of a culture problem statement may be: "Our teams need incentives to collaborate effectively because our current culture enables competition and favoritism."

Anticipating Inflection Points in Your Culture Transformation

Part of defining your action plan is identifying the change levers and key partners that will bring culture transformation to life. Peace Coffee's Lee Wallace told us that the healthiest cultures are not built purely top-down. She said, "I think it's top-down *and* bottom-up, and vertical *and* diagonal."[4] Culture must be designed with and for people cross-functionally at every level of the organization. Similarly, Paul Butler, a strategic leadership coach, adviser, and author, reminded us to think about scale when designing culture. Are you thinking at the level of team, business unit, or entire enterprise?[5] And if these discrete segments of your organization have different cultures, what will you do to create a cohesive vision for everyone? In his book *Think to Win:*

Unleashing the Power of Strategic Thinking (coauthored with John Manfredi and Peter Klein), Butler outlines several change levers, including those that are easier to push such as communication, policies, or recognition, and those that are harder to push, like organizational structure and rewards or compensation.[6] He recommends considering the impact, ease of implementation, time, and cost when considering which levers to push and why.

. . .

At this point as you define your intentions with culture, scaling your culture design is far off. Still, part of a thoughtful action plan is anticipating how your strategy will be affected both as it is cascaded throughout the organization and through your company's normal growth processes. Christa Quarles, CEO of productivity and design tool maker Alludo (and previously CEO of OpenTable), made the point that culture design must necessarily be different as a company grows.[7] She told us she felt there were breakpoints in organization size, at 50, 150, 500, 2,000, and 10,000 employees. At both Alludo and OpenTable, Quarles led significant culture transformations. She described the inherited cultures as "command-and-control," which, she said, were feasible only at a much smaller scale. She inherited both cultures at 600 to 800 employees, each of which had scaled from 50 or so employees. Quarles emphasized the importance for CEOs to understand what they really control in a culture. "You are not the culture. You're just the steward of the culture," she told us. That's why it's so important to keep your eye on what you *are* in charge of—like resource allocation and how people get rewarded. To unwind some of the ingrained behaviors she encountered, like fear of making mistakes, Quarles began rewarding growth-oriented behavior that required risk-taking. Her reward mechanisms included things like allocating more resources (e.g., hiring more engineers) or promoting people who were actively embodying change.

The Evolution of Our Culture Design Frameworks

As we've integrated James's operational experience with our learnings working with clients, we have developed a road map to design culture change. The steps are as follows:

1. Use action-learning principles and employee resource groups to drive business outcomes.

2. Create a highly intentional communication strategy.

3. Enlist key leaders as catalysts for change.

4. Reimagine and redesign your people strategy.

This road map applies to the Leaders Define the Reality step of the Culture Design framework by providing context for how to approach your action plan. While the steps were specifically related to creating anti-racist cultures, the principles are the same for any culture transformation. With some adaptations, we'll cover how they apply to defining your culture design action plan.

As we mentioned earlier, action-learning teams are a great tool to drive your desired outcomes, and utilizing diverse, cross-functional teams can maximize their contributions to the business. Employee resource groups can do so much more than plan events or serve as a safe space; they can also be leveraged for their unique vantage point on the organization and its opportunities for growth.

Once you've used one or a combination of tools to distill your findings and create your strategic road map, how will you share your vision and road map with the organization? Effectively communicating your plans is key to successfully getting everyone on board with the transformation, and an early chance to start modeling the culture through how you communicate it. You're going to want to communicate frequently and in many different modes (including symbols, rewards, and the other forms of communication we talked about in chapter 1). Don't underestimate how much repetition is needed for the message to sink in. Use the different mediums we have easily accessible to us—can you turn an email or intranet statement into a podcast, a short video, or even an infographic? How can you integrate your message into daily routines, like staff meetings?

It's important to keep in mind how you will tailor the message to different roles and functions. Your people will want to know what this culture change has to do with them. The role of a frontline employee will differ greatly from that of a marketing director or finance executive—and so will the information they need. Keep in mind both what they will need to do differently and how the shift will affect their work experience for the better. A personal touch is a great option where possible. One of our clients has been on a yearlong campaign to intentionally move the culture and drive their strategy. This CEO has been visiting each market to share the organization's vision with the employees and has been taking in feedback from each location. Setting up mechanisms for two-way communication will also help keep the flow of information active: if employees feel like there isn't space for feedback, they will be far less likely to embody the transformation you are creating. Your culture will not take hold.

Another aspect of communication to consider is creating a *shared language* to aid with transparency, collaboration, and conflict resolution. How can you create language that encourages discussion that is at once direct, honest, constructive, and respectful? Walking that line can be difficult. When James was at Nestlé Purina, a tool they used was called "speaking from the left-hand column." This was shorthand for "I'm about to say something that I would normally filter, but it is important to share." Creating simple language like that can help foster a more open and productive environment.

Getting key leaders from HR and middle management on board with your transformation strategy requires this kind of open and honest communication. You'll need to use the information you gathered during your culture audit to identify the people who will become the best champions of your change agenda. These include both formal and informal leaders who have a high level of trust and influence with their colleagues. You have to lay out your expectations clearly, as you will do in your tailored communications. What role do they play in this transformation? What input do they have? What new or shifting expectations do you have of how they work, lead, and collaborate? You'll also need to ensure that you provide the support, tools, and agency they need to advocate for change.

Distill your findings from the HR portion of your culture audit to determine where your culture needs to be reimagined. What should you start, stop, and continue doing? People or HR strategies touch everyone at a company and thus play a crucial role in culture throughout an employee's life cycle. This was one of the first parts of your audit and is often one of the first levers to pull as you envision your action plan. One way James has reimagined HR in previous roles was by implementing changes to the interview process. Adding in more unstructured, open-ended questions to work in concert with the standard ones can open up more information about candidates and bring insights about how they would enhance the culture you are designing. Whether you are adjusting the benefits package or tweaking how compensation is structured, always align these changes to what you've learned from talking to your people and to your overall strategy. Best practices are helpful guidelines, but the point of the work you did in the Leaders Empathize step was to lay the groundwork for you to understand your unique context.

Do What Matters

Each of these tools is intended to help you know what matters most to your company, strategy, and people. The intention here is not to overwhelm you with options but to give you a full arsenal of methods that you can tweak and adapt for your own use. All of this is leading to the implementation of your plan, when it is time to do what matters. In the next phase, you will want to use what you have learned, the vision you've set, and the plan you've made to support you as you move through the tasks you've set out for yourself. Everyone knows that what looks smooth on paper may come with bumps in practice. You will need to practice being adaptable without faltering from your core values and vision. The end matters more than the means.

Takeaways

- Use filtering tools to distill your findings from your culture audit.

- Define your vision using the future-back method.

- Set an action plan by working backward with what is possible in the future, rather than by using the limiting beliefs that have been in practice.

- Utilize action-learning teams to drive culture change.

- Enlist key HR, middle management, and cross-functional leaders as catalysts.

Part Two

Do What Matters

Chapter 3

Leaders Work the Plan

"Culture eats strategy for breakfast."

—Attributed to Peter Drucker

You've now got a full tool belt for your cultural transformation. During the Leaders Empathize step, you got into the minds of your workforce, understanding more deeply every system and process that touched people. You've read, researched, and asked questions. You've used proven tools to sift through your findings and collaborated on an action plan. You've laid the groundwork so that you can give yourself the best shot at successfully ingraining your redefined cultural values. Now, as the saying goes, ain't nothin' to it but to do it.

But once you start to do it, you'll be reminded of the fact that everything looks easier on paper. Knowing what matters, the steps of empathizing and defining, are times of optimism. It's hard work, for sure, but the progress shows up every time you find a gap that you need to fill and every experience in your company culture you hear about, whether it is an experience you want to preserve or one you want to eliminate. Think of those beautiful designers' and architects' renditions of new structures like cars, bridges, or stadiums. They are the product of the same design process we just outlined of understanding needs and defining what you're going to build. We all love to see those renditions; they are the idealized version of what we imagine in the real world.

Of course, getting those structures to live up to the plan is not easy, and it's the same for culture design. Once your plans are out in the 3D world, things will get messy, because humans are messy. Emotions, behaviors, and habits will get in the way. You'll need to work to align changes with key stakeholders, including middle management, your legal team, and your board. External events might throw a wrench into your plans. Luckily, there are some tools and strategies you can use to steel yourself in the face of these and other curveballs.

The strategies that follow will help ensure your culture design is as successful as possible given the challenges of the real world. How can you make what looks good in the plan you've designed work just as well in the day-to-day? Being open to feedback will help you remain agile in the dynamic reality of your business.

If you can get your plan deployed in the real world, though, there are great rewards in store, not the least of which is how your culture will become intentionally and inextricably tied to your strategy.

When James was at Jamba Juice, he had a hypothesis about the kind of culture required for the company to succeed, and he would continually test it through feedback from all his key stakeholders—

whether they were employees, customers, or his board—as well as the financial reaction to the performance and changes being made inside the company. Using a similar multipronged approach to collecting feedback allows you to adjust your plans as necessary while continuously integrating culture design with your overarching strategic goals.

Culture Stories from the Field: Winnebago Industries

At Winnebago Industries, the sixty-six-year-old outdoor recreation company, Vice President of Corporate Responsibility and Inclusion Jil Littlejohn Bostick helped the executive team lead a culture transformation during the pandemic that had a positive effect on the company's strategy. We were introduced to Littlejohn Bostick at the spring 2024 Chief Executives for Corporate Purpose Summit and were impressed by her background working on culture in companies at a global scale. We were also struck by her stories of Michael Happe, who as Winnebago's relatively new CEO led a journey to re-center the organization's cultural priorities to be more "people first." After more than a decade during which the company had not revisited its cultural artifacts, Winnebago's mission had become stale and lacked focus on comprehensive collaboration, making their values difficult to act on. Stale culture led to stale strategy. Centering the company's culture design around a people-first paradigm better aligned with evolving strategic priorities, like reaching wider audiences through a lens of inclusion. Happe's team needed to bring the company into the twenty-first century, shedding some of the stereotypes associated with RVs and similar equipment—namely: the misconception that only people from a particular ethnic or socioeconomic background enjoy the outdoors. The team started with revising their purpose and values to reflect this realignment. Their current purpose is "Elevating every moment outdoors."

A through line we've seen in great companies is their ability to connect to something that they can uniquely own and excel at. Your purpose needs to be something your people can rally around and act on. Digging in further, Winnebago's current guiding principles are "relentless excellence," "unparalleled collaboration," "purposeful innovation," and "exceptional experience." These principles show up in big strategic moves like the focus on sustainability, which has led to investments in product innovation like electric RV and boat prototypes. These investments are directly tied to the purposeful innovation and relentless excellence principles.

Finally, the values that direct Winnebago's daily actions are "Do the right thing," "Put people first," and "Be the best." The company has brought these values to fruition with initiatives like CommunityGO, its giving program that enables employees to donate their rewards to charities, showcasing how employee engagement and community connection have been embedded into the company's culture.

Winnebago's new purpose, principles, and values reflect the ways it had been evolving and help the company double down on a shift from profit first to people first.

To ingrain these values throughout the organization, Winnebago set out to shift the mindset and culture around what leadership means. The company defined a set of people- and collaboration-centered leadership expectations and considers all of its employees to be leaders. "If you are on the production line or the CEO, everyone's a leader," Littlejohn Bostick told us.[1] These expectations help set a clear focus on what matters in a company and again gives leaders something more concrete to wrap their heads around. Connecting culture and strategy back to purpose throughout the organization is what has made Winnebago's culture shift sustainable. Littlejohn Bostick believes that the biggest conflict in the "remote work versus on-site" debate was that leaders weren't thoughtful or purposeful in the aftermath of the initial pandemic-era crisis mode. Many leaders believe workers need to be in the office to be effective, but Littlejohn Bostick pointed out how remote work forces more intentionality in building culture—rather than falling back on a culture that develops by happenstance. She told us that culture not only connects to the company's strategy, it is the foundation of that strategy. "If you don't align it properly, then all of the initiatives and the plans and the goals that you're trying to meet will fail, right? You have to understand who you are, who your people are, what you're trying to achieve, how those different elements work together in order to be successful."

Its understanding of who it was—in other words, knowing what matters—guided Winnebago when it started doing what matters, such as integrating the strength of its legacy household brand with efforts to reach new audiences through investments in sustainability and by connecting to communities that have less access to the outdoors. As you implement your action plan, you should emulate Winnebago by keeping your eye on the long term.

Many readers will have experienced alignment effort firsthand through the growing pains of mergers and acquisitions. Littlejohn Bostick stressed the importance of thoroughly understanding the strengths of and collaborating with any acquired companies. One of Winnebago's acquisitions had such a strong relationship between employees and the division CEO that workers would quite literally sing to him as he walked the floor of the manufacturing plants. He had hired the first thousand employees personally. Had Winnebago injected itself into that subculture and forced it to conform right away to Winnebago's broader culture, it would have created a fraught situation. Littlejohn Bostick told us, "We try to work hard to not be Big Brother coming in and trying to make something happen, and so we do intentionally try to have conversations. Sometimes that means that it takes a little bit longer for things to shift, but only because we really truly want to get that buy-in versus that mandate." The extra time spent on empathy, understanding, and teamwork pays off in the long run.

To continuously nurture the health of its culture, Winnebago has instituted annual check-ins with its top sixty to seventy leaders with multiple days of intentional planning in addition to quarterly check-ins and an experience survey. These numerous touchpoints further ensure that the company is moving in the right direction and allow it to adjust when necessary. One final point that Littlejohn Bostick left us with is a reframe around team building. We have always felt that leaders should focus on culture *add* (the idea that employees can enhance culture with their unique skills and backgrounds) rather than culture *fit* (the status quo idea of "fitting in," which is good for group cohesion but can stagnate innovation) to enhance their organizations without homogeneity. Littlejohn Bostick agrees, likening the reframe to the difference between a salad and a melting pot. "You have your different types of lettuce, you have your different types of tomatoes, and cucumbers and onions, and you can see those different things. And when you put those things together, that's what makes the salad so amazing, right? . . . It doesn't lose who it is." Innovation happens when there are different voices in the room and everyone can bring their full selves to the table. When unique backgrounds, perspectives, and ways of thinking can stand out, everyone is pushed past their comfort zone to a growth edge, which is what great leaders are seeking in their teams.

Overcoming Growing Pains

Culture work must be dynamic. There are always surprises that come up as you start implementing. You'll feel the growing pains, manage learning curves, and face employee resistance. Many people aren't comfortable with change, even when it is change for the better. Any time you upset the status quo, there will be some push and pull. The work you did during the Leaders Empathize step—town halls, coffee chats, and other forms of two-way communication—shouldn't end now that you're starting to do what matters. The culture design process isn't linear; it's a dynamic, virtuous cycle. While implementing your culture change agenda, you need to build in feedback loops to keep you on track and course correct when necessary. Is there a shorthand or automated process you can use to understand your progress? An all-clear or alarm bell can be filtered through things like pulse surveys and can be as low-tech as a regular check-in with a select group of managers. Shared language can be helpful here; during James's time at Nestlé Purina, the company trained its leaders in skills and conditions for engagement, a set of guidelines and ideas such as "becoming 'truth savvy' and willing to explore the 'undiscussables'" or "respectful conflict" to build an environment of empathetic and direct communication. As we mentioned in chapter 2, they also used the shorthand "speaking from the left-hand column" (referring to certain thoughts we usually filter out due to fear or insecurity, as coined by Chris Argyris and Donald Schön and popularized by Peter

Senge[2]) to further encourage this expectation of candor. What's your own version of this? No need to reinvent the wheel here; it's likely an adaptation of a system you're already using.

From James's Notepad

One of our clients, a quickly scaling tech startup, recently brought me in to facilitate part of its executive leadership retreat. I led the participants through a lifeline exercise that had them map out the highs and lows of their entire lives. The CEO shared her life journey map with the entire executive team, and everyone also shared theirs in rotating pairs. The group of seven is already working more effectively together after getting a more vulnerable look at everything their colleagues bring to work. It opened siloed lines of communication and created opportunities for direct, respectful problem-solving.

The mechanisms you use to collect feedback will enable you to close the loop and respond to any sore spots and resistance that emerge in your culture work. Culture shifts often stall when employees don't feel that their needs and opinions are being taken into account, and they have less incentive to make any behavior adjustments. Some skepticism from your teams is healthy; it forces you to get square with what is most important during this realignment and why. Much as anticipating questions strengthens a speech or presentation, anticipating points of contention will improve your resolve and fuel momentum. Sam Bright, the vice president and general manager of

Google Play + Developer Ecosystem, told us that after reviewing anonymized surveys, he broaches some of the difficult topics in a follow-up meeting by asking and answering tough questions.[3] He stressed the importance of this type of strategy for trust-building and stands by the adage that trust equals consistency over time. He advised, "If you don't have time and you don't have consistency, then you need to really lean into vulnerability." Sometimes, you need to get your team on board quickly during a period of rapid growth, for example. Building trust through vulnerability and transparency can accelerate that process. Like the openness we talked about in chapter 1, practicing vulnerability as you do what matters is one way you can make progress on ingraining your culture design while contending with the realities of implementing changes in the 3D world.

At the same time, communicating your action plan persistently will help ingrain your culture, and it may take repeating yourself more often than you'd expect for people to get the message. Think about how many touchpoints it takes to close a sale. You've been on both ends of it—securing a key deal or doing something as mundane as clicking "purchase" after receiving an abandoned cart email. In the context of culture design, you're essentially doing two things with your communications: selling your teams on the vision and teaching people a new language of behavior. Whether you took Spanish or Mandarin in high school, you know it takes a while to internalize even the most basic of phrases. Your thoughtful communication through different modes (e.g., in a live meeting or speech, on a short video, in a podcast version of a blog post) is how you will get people to internalize and integrate the values and behaviors that enable your desired culture. We're going for depth of fluency here, rather than the satisfying but ultimately shallow quick hit of nailing your flashcards.

From Krista's Notes App

I have always loved learning languages. It is always most valuable to put in the extra time to learn the hows and whys of grammar—that way you can use critical thinking to come up with your own sentences rather than relying on a set of memorized phrases. Similarly, you want your employees to get to the place where they have ownership over the culture and find ways to live the values as a matter of course. As a leader, you may find it useful to dig into the words you're using and *why* and sharing those with people to deepen the connection. For example, you may have "transparency" as a core part of your culture. Lots of companies do, but if you can explain to people that you've thought about this word—which originates from a Latin word that meant "to show light through"—you can explain that's what your goal is. The modern definition, according to the online etymology dictionary, etymonline, is "presenting no obstacle to the passage of light, so that what is behind can be distinctly seen."[4] If my leaders told me this, I would remember that more than just a generic phrase about being transparent.

The trick to ingraining the behaviors required for the success of your culture design is finding a balance between patience, collaboration, and agility while also knowing when to draw a line in the sand. There are things you cannot compromise on, even in the most open, nonhierarchical environment. During his turnaround of Jamba Juice,

James laid out his plan and had to know when someone simply wasn't aligned despite an adjustment and feedback period. As he puts it, "Sometimes we've got to free up people's futures to go do something else as we carry on with the work." You also must find a balance between empathy for individuals and a commitment to the team, organization, and purpose as a whole. On one extreme, you end up treating people like expendable automatons; on the other, you may get bogged down with poor or inefficient behavior. You must always allow for people to absorb the change, but you cannot allow resistance to disrupt the team's progress. Hewing close to your values can help guide you through these sticky situations. An organization in the health-care industry may have a lower tolerance for production errors than, say, a publishing company. Whether you let someone go or they self-select out, you may well realize it had been a long time coming.

You may also encounter curveballs that feel more positive, like unexpected innovation. Building open and honest two-way communication allows for new ideas to shine through. As in the Leaders Empathize step, check your ego and assumptions about what will work. If someone seems on board with the new direction and has some additions or adjustments to suggest, they may help you unlock another layer of integration and real-world relevancy of your plan.

External Disruptions and Global Events

As we have all learned in the past few years, sometimes the hurdles we face are out of our control, hard to anticipate, and on a macro, not interpersonal, scale. There are times that big external conflicts or emergencies will make you feel at odds with you culture design plans, even as you try to implement them. Who cares about culture in the middle of a crisis?

We'd argue, though, that crisis is in fact what *defines* culture. In his previous role as chief product and experience officer at freelancer marketplace Upwork, Sam Bright led the first six months of his cultural rewiring on Zoom during the peak of the Covid-19 pandemic. Given the less-than-ideal circumstances, he couldn't take every action he would have in the pre-Covid world. One action he was able to prioritize was a virtual ugly sweater party featuring a remix of "'Twas the Night Before Christmas" that celebrated each of their product launches. It was creative and fun. But it isn't the specifics of that party that mattered—his team will remember the way they were recognized in a public, personal, and narrative-centered way. During a time of fear and isolation, that recognition is what mattered most in that moment.

Two of the guiding lights in these seemingly impossible situations are *Do what matters* and *Don't let perfect be the enemy of good.*

We titled the second part of our process Do What Matters because it is a simple, concise phrase that encapsulates how leaders should prioritize actions and behaviors as they navigate culture design in our messy, imperfect world. Nothing ever goes exactly to plan, and when things *really* don't go to plan, you must do what matters in that moment. Be it pandemic, war, natural disaster, or economic shock, having the agility to shift what matters most can make all the difference to the well-being of your employees and the people you serve. When Peace Coffee CEO Lee Wallace sent all but nonessential workers home during the pandemic, she was doing what mattered in that moment. The division between warehouse and office workers (who were now in different physical locations) was an element of the culture that had to be ad-

Leaders Work the Plan

dressed, but that would need to wait. Wallace was focusing on and underscoring the most important cultural element in that moment: safety and well-being. She made the choice that the situation required.

You may be thinking that while of course Wallace made the right decision in hindsight, what are you supposed to do when you've got stakeholders laying on the pressure to make choices that won't send the business spiraling in the long term? What if what matters most right now has a longer-term potential negative impact? We'd argue that ignoring what matters most right now out of fear of failure is what leads to long-term catastrophe. Decisions you make and actions you take on culture design have ripple effects that impact employee work experience as well as the quality and safety of your products and services. Sometimes these effects may be imperceptible—and like the slow drip of a leaky faucet, you may not notice until the floor caves in. In moments of crisis, it's your job to stop the leak. You can regrout the tile later.

An extreme example of how poor culture design prioritization can be catastrophic are the recent tragedies involving Boeing aircraft. A February 2024 Federal Aviation Administration (FAA) review found that the aviation giant had a poor culture of safety.[5] There was not only a breakdown of communication between executives and engineers, but there was also an explicit culture of profit over safety. The majority of manufacturing employees told investigators they had little to no faith that any safety concerns would be taken seriously. Higher-ups went so far as to threaten or imply retribution, amounting to a culture of "Shut up and get the product out as quickly as possible."[6]

But Boeing wasn't always like this. It was once one of the most well-respected companies in the United States, with a sterling reputation for safety and engineering excellence. For most of the twentieth century,

Boeing had an engineering-centric culture of innovation. Experts say the trouble started in 1997, when it merged with competitor McDonnell Douglas.[7] For the next twenty-five years, Boeing leadership would make a series of cost-cutting decisions that prioritized short-term profits over safety and progress. Ironically, in addition to the horrific loss of life resulting from these decisions, they also cost Boeing tens of billions of dollars in fines and lost profit in the long run.

While most companies don't have such high-stakes offerings as airplanes, there are many organizations where failing to do what matters has dire consequences. From outbreaks of foodborne illnesses, to exploding faulty smartphones, to homes lost due to unethical banking processes, our increasingly interconnected global economy requires cultures with a bigger emphasis on safety. Each decision these companies make can create far-reaching ripple effects throughout the supply chain.

"Don't let perfect be the enemy of good" is a twin to the sentiment "Do what matters." Although some situations (like engineering an airplane) do require obsessive perfectionism, you can generally still make progress on culture under less-than-ideal conditions. So if you face some unexpected obstacles, set your sights on what will be "good enough" right now. Always go back to your values to judge whether you are making progress in the right direction.

Jamba Juice had an extremely short time to turn the ship around. Before James joined the company, it had literally run out of cash and needed to be recapitalized or refinanced, and it needed to be in a mode where it was making *good* versus *perfect* decisions around strategy and culture. Even a perfectionist like James, who prides himself on getting things just right, had to contend with the knowledge that the company could refine its culture design over time. The company launched a new menu item, steel-cut oatmeal, in record time with fast-tracked research and testing within ninety days of James's arrival. It was a big hit, helping lift sales early on in his tenure, and was the first application of the desired results-centered culture.

From his decades of operational experience, previous research from the team, and clarity around what mattered most right then, James was able to be both decisive and thoughtful in a moment of crisis. This mindset was required for Jamba to win in the long-term.

Legal and Compliance Challenges

As organizations face challenges from externalities like legal or regulatory changes, supply chain disruptions or economic headwinds, they must sometimes become flexible with their culture change process. Legal risks have become particularly relevant of late as relates to anti-racist or DEI initiatives. Handling legalities while staying true to your values requires creativity. After affirmative action at colleges and universities was deemed unconstitutional in 2023, Krista's graduate school, Sarah Lawrence College, complied with the law while doubling down on its commitment to diversity: it added an application question that reads:

> In the syllabus of a 2023 majority decision of the Supreme Court written by Chief Justice John Roberts, the author notes: "Nothing prohibits universities from considering an applicant's discussion of how race affected the applicant's life, so long as that discussion is concretely tied to a quality of character or unique ability that the particular applicant can contribute to

the university." Drawing upon examples from your life, a quality of your character, and/or a unique ability you possess, describe how you believe your goals for a college education might be impacted, influenced, or affected by the Court's decision.[8]

We were impressed that instead of backing down from its commitments and values, Sarah Lawrence simply found a creative way to approach the issue, adhering to its culture. This is a great example of how to stay focused on the mission while responding to real-world challenges. Legal roadblocks can be frustrating, but they are par for the course. As you know, it's not the challenges you face but how you respond to them that define you as a leader.

Everett Harper, the founder and CEO of digital services firm Truss, always leans into the company's deeply ingrained values (build alliances; pay attention; show up, step up; pursue mastery; act without fear; be adaptable).[9] From the start, Harper focused on integrating culture with strategy by designing actionable values that the company lives every day. He spoke about escaping the trap that many corporations fall into, in which they create company values and mission statements that sound good on paper but lack any real connection to the business. "We had an explicit goal when we were trying to define explicitly our values and culture, that they had to be verbs because you didn't want anything that could be put on a poster with soft focus."[10]

Truss instead took one of the most diligent approaches we've seen to creating its guiding principles; in its first year of operation, the leadership team spent six 3-hour meetings hashing out these six values. This upfront investment paid off and continues to be reinforced thirteen years in, with consistent rituals like shout-outs at its all-hands meeting. The shout-outs are always tied to a way someone on the team is living one of Truss's values and creates an opportunity for each employee to own the culture. As a company with significant federal clients (it developed the successful project IRS Direct File, for example) Truss savvily navigates the real-time legal and regulatory changes and has held steadfast in its practice of working shoulder-to-shoulder with clients (one of the actions that embodies the "build alliances" value) to build software that works for everyone. This perspective serves both its clients and end users. This year alone, tens of thousands of Americans signed up for the software within the first few days of the 2025 launch.

Another great example of companies standing by their values amid compliance challenges is marketing and advertising amid social media censorship. Though Meta or TikTok's regulations are meant to create guardrails against illegal activity, wellness companies in cannabis and psychedelics (which stand on challenging legal ground at the federal level) and sexual health companies often find themselves struggling to get their Facebook ads approved. Through clever design and wordcraft that caters to those in the know, some companies find ways to serve a niche market by creating a sense of in-group exclusivity. Others lean into their values (such as reducing shame and a commitment to open expression) by directly calling on social sites to adjust their filtering systems. In chapter 1, "Leaders Empathize," we talked about how important branding, marketing, and public opinion are to your organization's culture. How are you seen in the world? What do your employees friends, families, and neighbors think about the workplace? Are they proud to say they work for you? Depending on your brand and the issue at hand, your response may not be as public or obvious as calling out a social media platform's policies, but you should always lean on your values when making tricky legal and compliance-related decisions.

Overcommunicate

As we mentioned earlier, creating systems for two-way communication is key during your culture change process. Everyone we have spoken to who has led a culture design has underscored how fundamental these feedback loops are. Timothy Escamilla, the CEO of legacy agriculture business Bolthouse Fresh Foods, told us he believes that every employee should have some sort of access to him, even if it's just to be heard for five minutes: "Those five minutes for you could be five minutes of a really busy day. However, for that person, it could be just five minutes of really getting off their chest ... and it sets them free. It enables them to get back to being productive."[11] This relates to Escamilla's unique perspective on culture, the primary role of which he views as "to reduce anxiousness by providing certainty about the vision for the future." This framing is unique and profound among top leaders as it even further centers the needs of the workforce. One of the reasons people are resistant to change is because of the uncertainty, so it's a great idea to acknowledge what your employees are going through and to provide clarity during a time that may feel turbulent. Certainty also creates trust. In times of instability, people create their own certainty. One way that shows up is through siloes, which are frequently indicators of a fundamental culture of mistrust. Siloing information can be a self-protective mechanism, and creating trust through certainty is one way to start to open the flow of communication back up.

The Honest Company's CEO, Carla Vernón, whose other title is Chief Dreams and Inspiration Officer, has ensured that she takes her team along with her throughout Honest's growth and change journey. As a leader to a relatively young workforce, she is mindful of the fact that many of her employees don't have a frame of reference for what to expect in times of change. "Never mistake chaos for creativity," she's said to her team in meetings.[12] Vernón has shared with her team her perspective that discipline is supportive of, rather than counter to, creativity, something she learned as a classically trained dancer. At the same time, she has talked them through the classic change curve, using the Pixar mood avatars we mentioned in chapter 1 as shorthand for the different stages people may be in throughout the process. Additionally, like Escamilla, Vernón keeps her door open by hosting "Ask Carla Anything" listening sessions to facilitate bidirectional listening and learning. This is the work of culture design in action—the doing what matters and tactics you should consider adopting.

Sam Bright pointed out the importance of communicating what you're doing and how it relates to the feedback you've received. He told us, "People don't always know that you are responding to their feedback when you do certain things. They can feel like they're not being heard. When they see that you're making an effort to respond to their feedback... then they can be like, 'Oh, okay, I feel like we're going in a particular direction.'"[13] Taking that extra step to not only remain transparent but also to connect back to the communications you've been having can reassure folks who may be resistant to or wary of changes. We were both inspired by the thoughtful and creative communications of these leaders, and you should take to heart their commitment to getting their message across multiple channels as they ingrain their culture design.

Documentation

Keeping good documentation is a sometimes-overlooked aspect of culture design and communication—but it's a gift to your future self and future employees. Whether it's there to formalize institutional knowledge for people five years down the road or to remind you what on Earth you did a month ago, documentation is a key tool for codifying and scaling change. Part of your job is to ensure that everyone is crystal clear on what their role is. As part of his turnaround of Bolthouse Fresh Foods, Timothy Escamilla took a critical look at who owned each strategic priority in the business. With clarity around each function, employees were liberated from playing the blame game as well as given ownership and accountability within the company. With this specificity, focus, and attention to detail, the organization saw big results: in just twelve months, it has turned a profit after years of losing money. It paid off for Bolthouse's people, too: the company had the lowest turnover in nine years. This work may not be easy, but it works.

Takeaways

- Expect a push and pull while implementing a culture transformation.

- Stick to your values and instincts to always do what matters in the face of challenges—this can have a huge impact on both your company and the lives of the people you serve.

- Think outside of the box when faced with external hurdles.

- Communicate continuously and consistently to keep everyone on the same page, and to build trust and certainty.

- Document what you're doing now to set up yourself and your team for the future.

Chapter 4

Leaders Iterate

"It isn't 10,000 hours that creates outliers, it's 10,000 iterations."

—AngelList cofounder and former CEO Naval Ravikant

By now you might be thinking, *I've done so much already—is there really more?* And look, we get it. The idea of cyclical, long-term work to build a culture on top of all your other daily operational tasks can seem overwhelming. You may feel like you've done enough. You may even feel fatigued, wondering if it's all worth it.

But you're a leader. Leaders don't quit, they iterate. Rest and reprioritize? Sure. Delegate? You betcha. But quit? No way. As you've been implementing the first phases of your action plan, you're likely already seeing some of the ways thoughtfully designing your culture reduces friction and changes the energy of the workplace. More smiles, laughter, and enthusiasm don't just make the day nicer—things like positive mood and momentum carry real, incremental, positive effects on productivity. Like many elements of culture, these are sometimes hard to see in isolation, and harder still to measure. Think of people who love New York City. They mention the world-class arts scene and wonderful restaurants, but almost every person will also mention the irrepressible electric rhythm of the Big Apple. That's not something you can easily point to or measure, but it's what keeps people coming back. So don't take your instincts for granted.

From Krista's Notes App

From the sky-high rents to the less-than-ideal weather, there are lots of reasons to leave New York City. But despite being raised in suburbs around the country as my father earned more and more high-level leadership positions, this city is the only place that's ever really felt like home. The *culture* of this city is right for me and still finding new iterations of itself. It has brought the best out of many artists, innovators, business owners, and dreamers. Likewise, pairing the right culture with the right people is what will make your organization reach new heights. When designing culture intentionally, you do not force a New York City on a team of St. Louisans. Conversely, you do not cater to the comfort of where your people are at the moment. This is the hard work of culture design, creating meaningful lasting change that doesn't feel foisted on the organization but also pushes toward a new, better place.

Your gut—which has led you through tough negotiations, difficult cost-cutting measures, and securing career-making promotions—will sense that the shifts you're making to shape the culture are having an impact long before the change shows up in the data. Keep going.

Whether your bumps in the road to this point have been small or they've thrown you for a loop, you've learned invaluable information about how your culture works in the real world. As anyone who's spent time in formal classroom settings can tell you, six weeks of work experience can sometimes teach you more than years of study. But it's that study—in this case, your diligent work to empathize with your workforce and define your plan—that sets you up for exponential growth. Iteration is a huge part of the design thinking process, and for good reason. The rapid iteration phase allows designers to quickly incorporate user feedback to refine their product, turning big bets into a series of smaller, easily adjustable bets. This cuts down on time, money, energy, and risk and leads to a better end result.

So, just like we would if we were building an app or a new kind of backpack, we will iterate on the work of designing culture. Creating space for experimentation involves thoughtfully and methodically testing different tactics to shape your culture and can include multi-tiered road maps to culture change, with each level building on the last. To be clear, though, *no* version of culture design iteration will be throwing spaghetti against a wall and seeing what sticks. You will draw on all the groundwork you've done thus far to act on a structured, well-informed hypothesis.

Let's look in detail at several leaders' approaches to iteration in their culture design. These examples are from companies in various industries, of different sizes, and in a range of growth stages. As you read, think about which tactics fit with where you are in your strategic goals, and where you can adjust ideas for your industry or the size of your company. Don't discount methods used by leaders of companies vastly different from yours. For example, early-stage startups have something to teach mature enterprises about agility, while global companies provide newer organizations with a road map for utilizing strong systems and processes.

What Iteration Looks Like

Sometimes iterating on culture design means building directly on the empathy and vulnerability you've already been flexing. Throughout his entire career, Sam Bright has methodically focused on experimentation in his approach to building intentional cultures. Early on at Google, where he led the fast-growing team that focused on Google Play and its developer ecosystem, he used a tool called a "personal user manual." It's a clever take on tech user manuals, which Bright now simply calls his About Me. Bright creates an in-depth document that gives teams the shorthand they need to get to know him. By including the personal (guilty pleasures), the professional (the best ways to reach him), and the intersection of the two (how his background affects his leadership style), Bright's About Me models empathy and gives his large, distributed team an inside look into him as a full person.

While the About Me was a great way to build bidirectional empathy, he felt it could still go a little deeper. So he iterated. Encouraged by a mentor, Bright also began sharing his Journey Line with his team. This document presents more of a narrative, timeline-style overview of what made him the man and leader he is today. "People won't always go and reference your About Me or what have you, but they will start to remember the stories that you've told," he said.[1] Giving people more context further opened the door for connection and sharing between himself and the team and among team members themselves. This helped solidify a foundation of empathy that is paramount to the cohesive team culture Bright was intentionally creating.

As we mentioned in chapter 3, James recently led the leadership team of one of our clients through a lifeline exercise. The lifeline is a bird's-eye view of your life journey, created in a similar way to Bright's Journey Line. This process involves plotting key personal and professional highs and lows, as illustrated in the next section. James has been using the lifeline exercise for twenty-plus years to build empathy and trust and drive culture. We now also use this exercise with teams trying to build trust and stronger cultures with our Culture Design Lab clients.

James D. White Lifeline

When going through his lifeline, shown in figure 4-1, James shares the highs (like the births of his daughters and his first VP promotion) and the lows (like his prostate cancer diagnosis and the loss of his mother) and describes how they have shaped him, his values, and his leadership style. It helps people get to know him and opens the door for others to share, too. Sharing his life journey always allowed James to build trust and agility across the organization. The iterative nature of the Jamba turnaround was aided by his openness and transparency with the team.

FIGURE 4-1

James D. White's lifeline exercise

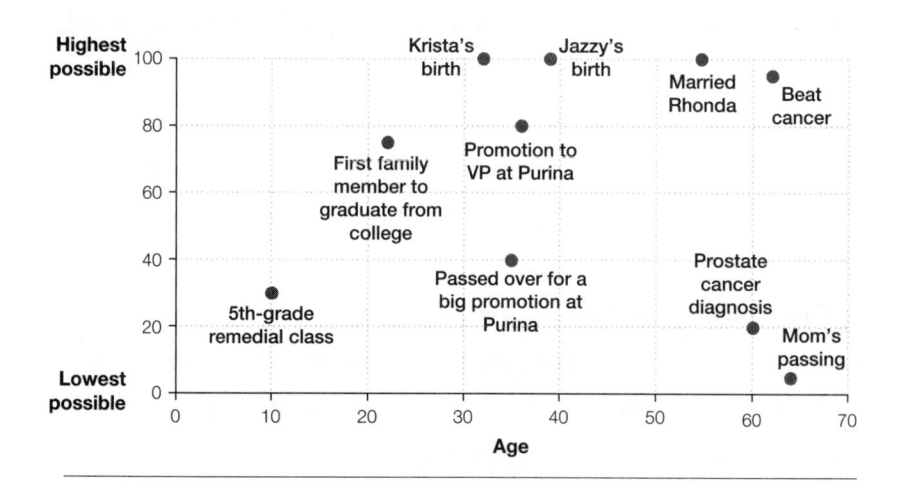

Age	Event	Rating
~10	5th-grade remedial class	30
~22	First family member to graduate from college	75
~32	Krista's birth	95
~35	Promotion to VP at Purina	80
~36	Jazzy's birth	95
~37	Passed over for a big promotion at Purina	35
~55	Married Rhonda	95
~58	Prostate cancer diagnosis	40
~60	Beat cancer	95
~63	Mom's passing	10

(Y-axis: Lowest possible (0) to Highest possible (100); X-axis: Age 0 to 70)

✏️ From James's Notepad

Through the years, I have iterated on my leadership style to integrate more of my full humanity. This wasn't something I started with at all. I came up in a business culture that expected us to be one way at work and another way at home. I can see now, and have learned much from Krista, who has never been part of a workforce that didn't accept at least some integration of "work self" and "life self." While there are of course always professional boundaries, I've come to believe that sharing important parts of my life's journey has made me a more human—and more effective—leader. It helps people understand where I am coming from and relate to those around me on a deeper level. And even when this felt uncomfortable, I learned from Krista just how much the younger generations now filling the workforce believe—and indeed expect—that leaders should be fully human at work and should honor their desire to be the same.

As for Sam Bright, he spends a *lot* of time listening to long-tenured employees. This allows him to come into their world with a sense of what will work with this combination of people. His conversations have brought insights into subtleties such as how to frame communication so that the team will resonate with it instead of bristle at it because, say, it was accidentally similar to a prior negative communication from leadership. Another conversation may cause him to iterate on rituals he wants to introduce into team meetings. Context is the key here—the history of a team plays a crucial role in how a tactic will be received. During this phase, you're leveling up the groundwork you laid out in the Leaders Empathize step and using those skills to not only build two-way empathy but also to refine how you ingrain your desired culture.

As we mentioned in Leaders Define the Reality, James's turnaround at Jamba Juice ultimately involved a three-part culture design plan, Blend 1.0, Blend 2.0, and Blend 3.0. (Yes, the blender reference is an intentional nod to Jamba's hallmark smoothies.) But in the beginning, these phases were just called the Blend Plan. As we mentioned in chapter 3, James knew he had to act quickly, focusing on good over perfect to get the company out of the danger zone. So he turned to iteration on the Blend Plan, which became three phases. Between cash reserves strained by rapid growth and the onset of the greatest financial crisis in eighty years, Jamba was in trouble. James strengthened his executive team and set forth with what would become Blend 1.0:

Financial Turnaround. The crucial first year on the job taught him that a focus on culture, values, and disciplined, collaborative behaviors had to be omnipresent for the company's success. He knew from the outset that his culture design, right alongside his strategy, would be iterative. The plan was built to be responsive, to make the company more resilient and sustainable, and to weather the challenges of the marketplace with the goal of winning with the customers. James's focus was to get the company back on the rails while returning to consistency in operational excellence. From refranchising a significant number of company-owned stores to redesigning the cups so the company could eliminate two ounces of waste for every twenty-four-ounce smoothie, this focus on details changed how employees at every level showed up. Getting back to the core values that had made the business so special in the first place created a positive feedback loop—James's strategic decisions emphasized a culture of innovation and efficiency, while behavior changes fed into the company's progress.

The detail orientation also showed up in the retooled systems and processes, like the enterprise software that replaced spreadsheets and allowed teams to review operating results at each store daily. Leveraging technology and automation allowed adjustments to be made at the speed of external change and ultimately reduced general and administrative expenses by 30 percent in roughly two years. Notice here how culture is being driven by operational decisions and technology, not just conversations and statements about purpose and vision. Those things, as we've discussed, are crucial, but there is a tactical aspect of building culture that emerges out of the way you conduct business and iterate on the changes you're making. Being able to review results daily in-store might not be what you associate with building a strong, intentional culture, but in this case, it was a core part of giving workers a sense of ownership and understanding of what the company stood for—accountability and empowering frontline workers.

Consumer packaged goods licensing agreements implemented during Blend 1.0 also created new revenue opportunities for Jamba Juice, and this segment of the business was further refined during Blend 2.0: Strategic Turnaround, a period beginning in 2012. By the end of 2012, through international expansion to Mexico, the Philippines, and South Korea as well as four hundred self-serve JambaGo stations and the resurgence of a rigorous testing cycle, Jamba turned a profit for the first time in six years.

During Blend 3.0: Transformative Growth, which extended through 2013 and beyond, Jamba continued to see increased operating profit margins, store-level margins, and expansion of their franchise program. None of this would have been possible without the culture that James and his team meticulously designed and continuously refined, centering on empathy within the organization and, crucially, for the consumer.[2]

The change and turnaround work at Jamba was the reflection of James's own growth as a leader starting as a first-time CEO. It also reflects the change in leadership capability of the team and the investment they made in culture over time. They prioritized culture design from day one, iterated throughout his time there, and invested in it through James's last day at Jamba. Toward the end of his eight years with the company, James did some of the most robust action-learning work to ensure that the positive culture changes he and his team had invested in were sustainable beyond any individual leaders. His tenure cemented how strongly he feels about a leader's role as they transition out of a company. It's far more personal than succession planning; it's about legacy.

Strategy is always at the forefront, inextricably linked with culture in successful iterative processes, with the goal to intentionally design culture and create great organizations. One company we worked with was an early-stage tech company. The CEO was rapidly scaling her seventy-five-person company, preparing for the organization to roughly double in size in a short period of time. After the startup's recent IPO, the CEO had a few major priorities. She wanted to scale the company thoughtfully as she built out her leadership team. She knew there was an acute need to focus on culture, people, and values. She also knew that there needed to be some refinement as she had moved from a fifty-person organization that had grown by 50 percent in a relatively short six-month period and would double again over the next twelve to fifteen months. She brought us in as one of the external resource partners to coach her through flexing and stretching her own leadership capabilities as well as thinking through processes and tools that would allow her to fine-tune and adjust her culture as the company scaled.

As she reached a growth breakpoint, this startup CEO realized that her leadership style was too micromanaging. Founders tend to have an "It has to get done right" and "I'll do it myself" mindset, but that doesn't work at scale, and her employees were starting to feel the squeeze. We focused on building systems that allowed her to get more feedback, which we framed as: "What should we start doing, what should we stop doing, and what should we continue doing?"

After gathering those responses, the CEO implemented a core process that would bring the most senior layers of leadership into a series of two-day quarterly review meetings. In addition to the usual reviews of strategy and financials, half of this protected meeting time would be spent tying the quarter's successes and challenges to the vision of the organization—how it planned to grow and scale, and a refinement around values and how the organization would get built out moving forward. These continuous feedback mechanisms must be implemented and fine-tuned, just as they were at the start of putting your action plan to work. They allow for leaders to remain agile and to move at the pace of change.

For our CEO, structure and process refinements needed to happen from a leadership perspective, and one of the critical challenges was how to scale her own leadership and delegate as the company was growing. She created a series of action-learning processes to tackle the hairiest problems within the company and then broke her leadership team into groups of three or four, so small groups could work on the same problem, each from different angles, throughout the quarter. The intention with these action-learning teams was twofold: to leverage the full capability of the leadership team to help her solve bigger problems and to have the teams learn to work with each other cross-functionally, which would build capacity as the organization continued to scale and intentionally inject a culture of cross-discipline collaboration.

James encouraged her to use action learning, because like at Jamba, he could see that this company and CEO could benefit from the way cross-functional groups accelerate problem-solving and iteration. This CEO also fostered her capacity for open-mindedness around bi-directional communication. She used surveys that were distilled for leaders, who in turn worked on values and culture inside their respective functional areas of the team. This was a multi-month process that will continue as the business grows. Over time, these refinements have allowed the organization to measure where the team had been successful in changing behaviors and delivering better results and more aligned communication, so that she could continue to strengthen and build the culture in coming months and years.

Mike Slessor, the CEO of semiconductor industry leader FormFactor, also told us about the importance of creating consistent feedback loops to iterating and sustaining his culture. Though he describes himself as "a little late to the culture game," he has spent the past few years fully dedicated to transforming the health of his culture. Slessor credits his CHRO chief human resource officer, Aliza Scott, with opening the organization's eyes about how to lead at scale. He quickly committed to investing in culture. One way he continuously receives feedback from throughout the organization is through his twice-monthly fireside chats focused on values and culture. These virtual chats include an update from Slessor, a guest speaker from within or external to the organization, and, importantly, a ten-minute anonymous Q&A. He gets to hear from a broad set of people from his two-thousand-person organization, and they gain ownership over the culture. He also models accountability with his chats—in the five years since he has implemented them, he has never canceled one. The consistency and diligence involved in conducting more than a hundred culture-focused chats show the kind of dedication required for deeply thoughtful iteration.

Iterating on your culture design requires a persistence and attention to detail that so often falls to the wayside amid the pressures of rapid growth. It's why so many companies end up (with varying degrees of success) hiring CEOs tasked with recovery and renewal. The new CEO of a midsize retailer we worked with recently came into his job with a challenge like the one James faced at Jamba Juice in 2008. The company's core values and foundational products were strong, but after a number of leadership blunders and inconsistency in both branding and operations, the organization was flagging. This CEO quickly focused on the areas necessary to start running a tighter ship, including operational excellence, aligning with a sales-focused culture, and developing talent and efficiency. Again, we see how leaders iterate by meticulously tying culture design to strategy, often by embedding sustainable systems and processes throughout their plans. This CEO created what essentially amounted to an annual plan to transform the company through planned iteration. It broke down as follows:

- Phase 1

  - Complete a business process reengineering session with particular focus on profitability and training of associates on what matters.

  - Conduct a brand, product, and pricing study.

  - Hold a leadership conference to align top layers of team.

- Phase 2

  - Use phase 1 learnings to relaunch product offerings.

  - Reimagine brand.

  - Build on training on what matters to onboard streamlined facilities program.

- Phase 3

  - Put in place a comprehensive communication plan to continue iterating on open, cross-functional collaboration.

- Implement feedback and measurement system to enable continuous culture design iteration this year and beyond.

- Refine and evolve culture design based on learnings from first two phases.

This is a good model to borrow if you're looking at how to think about iterating on your culture design. The CEO's plan was tailored to his company (especially in some of the details we've left out for privacy reasons), but the basic outline and priorities are comparable to James's work at Jamba Juice and many other turnaround stories. They boil down to a rigor and discipline around context and detail that enables streamlining. This goes back to doing what matters. The zoomed-out view of what needs to be done may be incredibly simple, and it's the intense study of a business and its stakeholders that allows leaders to choose the right, simple priorities. Iteration helps leaders identify those priorities and rapidly adjust as needed so they can do what matters amid an ever-changing world. Iteration allows leaders to methodically manage culture as they strive to improve overall performance of their business.

The Continuum of Change

Iteration necessarily involves periodic and sometimes frequent change, and even when the tweaks are small, it can be a challenge for everyone to feel like they are on solid ground. Great leaders can create a foundation of certainty and stability, even amid change. This foundation will also further ingrain your culture design by fostering trust in your intentionality and commitment. Communicating classic models

FIGURE 4-2

The change curve

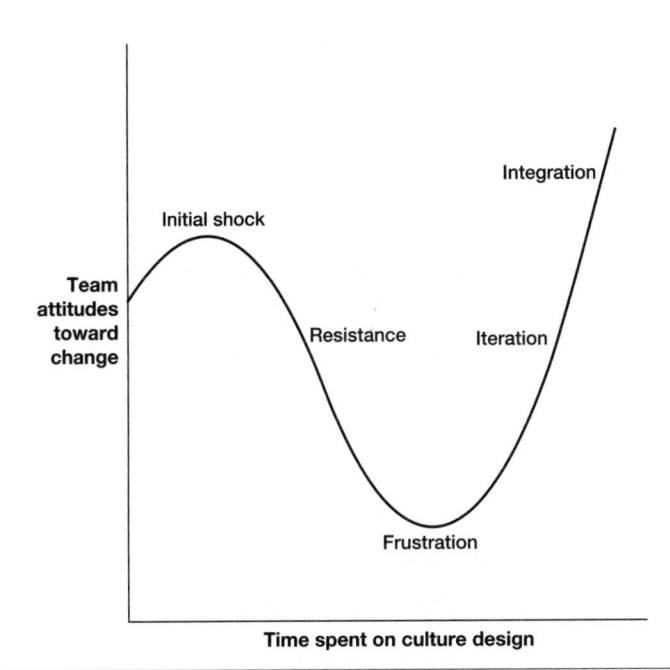

[Chart showing team attitudes toward change (y-axis) over time spent on culture design (x-axis). The curve starts with "Initial shock" at a peak, descends through "Resistance" to a trough at "Frustration," then rises through "Iteration" to "Integration."]

of change like Bruce Tuckman's model (forming, storming, norming, and performing) or Cynthia Scott and Dennis Jaffe's change model (denial, resistance, exploration, and commitment), can help frame expectations during times of disruption, and for visual learners, the so-called change curve can be a helpful reminder that change is a nonlinear process (see figure 4-2).[3] In addition to transparency around your plans and iterations, being up-front about the way your team may experience change is also a helpful way to meet people where they are. Within both these change models, there are supportive frameworks to help you respond to different stages. With the forming/denial stage, you can lean into active listening and providing clarity.

You can support your people through the discomfort and tension of storming/resistance by continuing to communicate regularly and by remaining positive, patient, and direct. Encouragement and acknowledging small wins can build momentum in the norming/exploration phase, while the performing/commitment phase requires focus, delegation, and continued check-ins.

Creative tension, as described by Peter Senge, is the energy created in the space between vision and the current reality.[4] How do you encourage your employees to hold this tension as energy and momentum rather than an untraversable chasm? Acknowledge the feelings they are experiencing in the present or may feel throughout the culture change process. Change can come with excitement, motivation, and renewed energy, and it can also come with fear, anxiety, worry, and resistance—sometimes all in the same week. While corporate leaders may be used to providing a motivational-speaker brand of positivity, acknowledging the full range of emotions you and your team may feel can help alleviate stress. Have you ever called a friend and said, "Can I vent for a second?" Or does your spouse tell you "It's completely normal and fair to feel overwhelmed when you've been working so hard"? How did you feel in those situations? We'd guess a lot better than when people tell you that everything is fine or gloss over your emotions. Everyone wants to feel validated, and understanding the different stages of change will help you empathize with your team as well as treat your own emotions respectfully during this process. Some of the emotions workers and even customers may go through as you iterate on our culture design include: self-protection and defensiveness, pessimism and resistance, anxiety and fear, sadness, anger, excitement and energy, and contentment, focus, and calm.

Feelings are often seen as these soft squishy things that get in the way of business and professionalism. And while of course there is a time and place for everything, it's OK to bring the fullness of your humanity into the workplace. You also don't need to make moves to fix or change anything if strong emotions come into play. Acknowledge and validate, but don't jump right into action mode. People need time to sit in their feelings around change and adjust to their new normal. Often, given a little time to ride it out, teams will settle in just fine. Preparing yourself and your teams for the continuum of change will make implementing your iterations more seamless and will help you glean more productive learnings and feedback from each refinement in your culture design plan.

Culture Stories from the Field: The Bay Club

The Bay Club, the high-end brand of West Coast sports, fitness, and hospitality clubs (James is on the board) has had to respond to societal and technological shifts many times throughout its forty-five-year history. As it has remained steadfast in its commitment to improving its members' health and well-being, its most recent cultural adjustment period began during the pandemic, when the company made an intentional decision to reshape its culture. "Companies change and grow, and we said it's time . . . we brought all different levels of leadership together over a six-month period, and had meetings and dove deep into what I would consider our DNA," Bay Club CMO Tracy Cioffi told us.[5] This deep dive, which is effectively the archaeological dig we outlined in chapter 1, led to a redefined set of principles, which the company calls "actions we live by":

- Keep it real always.

- Stay humble. Hustle harder.

- Think ahead. Be an owner.

- One team. One voice. Moving forward together.

- Stay curious. Ask why.[6]

This refresh was the first values revision in twelve years, with the second action particularly connecting to the company's blue-collar DNA. No one is too good for any job at the Bay Club, and the company values a gritty, egalitarian work ethic. CEO Matthew Stevens, who started his career in the then-nascent fitness industry working the front desk at sports club, told us "Never forget what it's like to work on the front lines . . . We ground ourselves in that concept of 'don't ask anybody to do anything you won't do yourself.'" This creates perspective for people at every level and builds empathy among coworkers in different functions.

For more than fifteen years, Stevens has led the Bay Club with a nod to one of his favorite leaders—not an athletic coach, like many of his colleagues, but one of the innovators who has long represented the best of Silicon Valley: Steve Jobs. The text of the iconic "crazy ones" speech narrated by Jobs in Apple's original "Think different" commercial hangs as a framed poster in several places around the Bay Club HQ. It is a reminder of the open-source, collaborative leadership Stevens has always brought to the table. He is "a rising tide lifts all boats" leader, passionate about paying it forward for the greater good through internships, apprenticeships, and information-sharing with others in the field. The Jobs poster also reminds the team to swing big.

One big swing the Bay Club took amid this cultural refresh was a pandemic-era iterative process to launch a new kind of membership at its clubs. For decades, the fitness industry had been selling family memberships—with restrictions as to who could be considered "family." As our ideas of kinship have shifted over the years, it became clear to the Bay Club team during the peak of Covid that they needed to rethink how they conceived of these group memberships. They chose to pilot a membership with more customization that allowed members to choose up to five additional people they wanted as part of their plan, as well as what features they'd like to include. The Bay Club iterated on the design of this program and, as it refined it, incrementally increased the number of pilot memberships from 250 to 500, and so on. Now these plans are the default sign-up option for the Bay Club's 100,000-plus members. The iterations it made with its culture design enabled this willingness to take a risk on a category-redefining idea. Risk-averse cultures may feel "safe" in the short term but being willing to fail and make mistakes is what creates big wins in the long run. When they are calculated and well considered, these risks and experiments have the best chance at success.

Iterations like those run by the Bay Club allow organizations to build their tolerance for risk as well. While the phased implementation of the new membership model ingrained and encouraged a culture of calculated risk-taking, the *content* of the memberships underscored values around community, family, and social bonds. The Bay Club sees both members and associates as part of a community, so this move incrementally brought the community values more into the real world. Both the act of iteration itself and the *what* you will iterate on have distinct and useful impacts on accelerating your culture design. As leaders iterate, culture meets strategy.

Takeaways

- Iteration is a mark of a great leader.

- Rigorous attention to detail creates the space for flexibility and experimentation.

- Planning phases that build upon one another provides a framework of stability and certainty.

- Bringing your employees along throughout the continuum of change can help ease friction during iteration.

- Leaders seek feedback and overcommunicate.

- Immersion in the experiences and needs of the frontline workforce is a hallmark of thoughtful leaders.

Chapter 5

Leaders Bring Culture to Life

"Alone we can do so little; together we can do so much."

—Helen Keller

If you're following the design thinking process we've been laying out so far, by now you've likely spent a lot of time with your senior leadership team iterating on your culture design. You may see promising results throughout the company. But culture varies by level, job function, and business unit. How can you highlight the strengths of each team while also maintaining a cohesive overall culture? How can you ensure that efficiency, innovation, and employee engagement doesn't suffer in less senior roles? Middle managers lead, implement, and shape culture, while the culture lives with the frontline workers. This chapter is about operationalizing your culture design and helping the organization live and activate its values. It is time to put those systems, rituals, and processes you've developed to work as you fully activate the behaviors that sustain your culture.

Bringing your culture to life throughout the company in sustainable ways means, above all, engaging middle managers and the frontline and entry-level workers they manage. We need to look at the difference between equity and equality here. Building a great company for all doesn't mean everyone has the same experience at work (equality). It means that the *quality* of the experience is the same (equity). For some people, childcare benefits or additional paid time off might hold more value than other types of recognition and celebration like the much-maligned pizza party. (Although for the record, we don't think there's anything wrong with a well-placed pizza party, especially if there's pepperoni.) Likewise, the types of training you offer to bring the culture to life will vary depending on function. Employees at your manufacturing plant may have less time and flexibility to complete a video course on your company's leadership values, but maybe there's a way to integrate key learnings into their daily safety briefing. This equality-versus-equity distinction allows you to find ways to include and integrate people throughout the entire organization instead of neglecting those who have different needs than the people in your corporate headquarters.

When we use the phrase "bringing culture to life," we mean integrating your groundwork and iterative implementation to fully activate your culture design at every level of the organization. This phase of intentional culture design is about scaling and solidifying the behaviors that create a cohesive, high-performing organization. It's about bringing your plan to life in the way that best matches the needs of the specific group you're targeting. The best companies and leaders engage middle managers in their crucial roles as the culture builders that can execute here. Their buy-in is required for the continued success and longevity of your culture and vision. Without the full participation of middle managers and frontline workers, the best-laid plans will flounder. But by continuously investing in them, you will see the culture you've designed thrive and even transcend the bounds of any individual senior leader. With them, culture reaches its true form, leaping off the page to become a living, breathing force in your organization.

So how can you bring everyone along for the ride while continuing to scale and integrate your culture design? VP of Google Play + Developer Ecosystem Sam Bright has dealt with this challenge throughout his career, especially as it relates to merging large teams. He stresses the importance of embracing uniqueness, saying "We're not a blob team. We each bring different components of our culture to then form this broader culture that enables us to be successful in being there for developers, just as they are experienced in building apps and then trying to scale and monetize them . . . Those dimensions are how we are forming the culture."[1] In addition to the experimentation that we mentioned in chapter 4, Bright also gives his team opportunities to sign up for fifteen-minute office hour slots to talk about any questions, ideas, or concerns they may have. He supplements traditional engagement surveys by creating bespoke surveys that ask deeper and more targeted questions to pinpoint what's resonating with the team. Use personalized tactics like Bright's custom surveys to add dimension to the data from your more standardized pulse and engagement surveys. The difference here might be as simple as tweaking the statement "At work, my opinions seem to count" to read "My opinions on our latest product launch were heard and valued."

In developing a more regular and evolving understanding of your people, especially on large, dispersed teams, you can gain insight into how to integrate your culture thoughtfully across the company.

But middle managers have historically been a tricky demographic to engage. Between exponential advancements in automation, financial crises, and a pandemic, middle managers have suffered disproportionately from layoffs. Whether they've lost their jobs or have ended up overworked and burned out, these key players have been underutilized. In *Power to the Middle: Why Managers Hold the Keys to the Future of Work*, authors Bill Schaninger, Bryan Hancock, and Emily Field argue that middle managers have at times been perceived as the immovable or frozen layer of management not because they are inherently ineffective, but because they have been squeezed into so small a space that they are holding on to siloed communication and bloated bureaucracies for dear life.[2] Similar to Timothy Escamilla's description of communication blockades that stem from uncertainty and mistrust, these conceptions about middle managers are in fact symptoms of a misaligned culture. To realign middle management with your purpose and values, you need to get clear on both what makes a great middle manager and what conditions need to be present for them to succeed as your partners in culture design. These factors ultimately lead to their success in their jobs and cascade to a stronger, more effective organization. In our work, we always view middle managers as the big unlock to bring culture to life.

From James's Notepad

Throughout my career as an executive in consumer products, retail, and restaurants, I have always made a point of experiencing what the frontline's daily reality is like. My first job was as a busser at my hometown burger joint, and that service industry experience came full circle as I led Jamba Juice. Whether I was learning what it was like to make smoothies during the lunch rush or helping wash dishes in the back, getting a glimpse of the in-store realities has always helped me re-center on what mattered most at a company—our employees and ultimately our customers. This might seem like an obvious thing for a leader to do, but many of the clients we work with don't engage enough with the front lines. The value of bringing the culture you're designing directly there is that it creates two-way infusion of the culture: from the top down and the bottom up. Add in having middle management as a direct line of communication for leaders to infuse the culture, and you have a kind of omnidirectional culture design—from the top down, the bottom up, and the middle out. If you hope you can design the culture and just let it seep down from the top leadership, it's not likely to work.

Culture Stories from the Field: Far Niente

When Dirk Hampson joined Far Niente Winery as a young assistant winemaker, Napa Valley was still a scrappy little wine region and the winery he would eventually run as CEO and chairman was just a few years old. (The 1970s incarnation of the winery was a revitalization of the original Far Niente, started by winemaker John Benson in the 1880s. By the 1970s, it had been defunct for decades.) James met Hampson, now a legend in the Napa wine industry, at a leadership retreat. As they got to know each other, James was impressed by

Hampson's intentionality and commitment throughout four decades to always focus on culture by cultivating his middle managers and frontline employees. From groundskeepers to winemaker apprentices, all the way up to his senior leadership team, Hampson was dedicated to giving people the tools they needed to succeed, which in turn made them stronger ambassadors of his culture design.

Coming on board as the winery's fourth employee, Hampson had the opportunity to truly design culture from the ground up. Working at European wineries for a couple of harvests had cemented his love for the craft. His apprenticeships had also given him perspective on legacy and long time scales, elements that were inherent to both the nature of wine and the way these centuries-old wineries thought about the craft. Fine wine is a quality-over-quantity business, and Hampson, along with founder Gil Nickel and the other original members of the team, were always clear on their vision of becoming one of the world's greatest wineries. That long-term guiding light was underpinned by a single powerful value: do the right thing. In other words: do what matters.

Through Hampson's next forty years with Far Niente, the company grew from a four-person operation making one wine to a group of five wineries with two-hundred-plus employees and dozens of outstanding wines. Distilling its culture down to "do the right thing" guided Far Niente through the many inflection points it faced through the decades, including expansion, restructuring, and the passing of Gil Nickel. But Hampson stressed to us that "do the right thing" has never meant "don't make mistakes." On the contrary, when everyone has buy-in to the mission, it creates the trust needed for teammates to be willing to fail. Our society is set up to be risk-averse, but you must take chances to innovate, improve, and grow. Trust played a role in

Leaders Bring Culture to Life

how Hampson thought about consumers as well. Spending $100 on a bottle of wine requires a great deal of trust in a company. "We weren't trying to just be efficient. We were trying to make *our* wine. We were trying to make Far Niente. We weren't going to be all things for everybody. Therefore, we could be the very best at being ourselves."[3] He invested in that long-term buy-in by modeling a culture of leadership, accountability, and continuous teaching and learning. His middle managers and frontline workers not only became more effective at their jobs by developing leaders behind them but also would at times rise to senior leadership themselves, enabling them to take part in a virtuous cycle of expanding the original vision.

As the company grew, many of the employees ended up staying with Far Niente for decades. The team realized early on, after giving a departing team member a Rolex as a gift for twenty years of service, that they also needed to be rewarding people while they were still there. Now, they celebrate milestones like year one, year five, and so on. And every employee who hits that twenty-year mark still gets to pick out their own luxury watch. The first people to inaugurate this new tradition were three groundskeepers—who all chose matching gold watches.

Hampson's commitment to fostering internal opportunities for growth stems from how his multiple roles throughout the years allowed him to grow as a leader and winemaker. When we asked about his hiring and training of people internally to rise to the highest levels of winemaking and selling, he told us, "If me having a number of roles was worthwhile, then isn't it worthwhile for other people to have a number of roles? The imagination to allow somebody to go into an area where he or she isn't proven or tested necessarily is something that a good leader can encourage—sometimes require."

This approach to building a deep bench within an organization ties back to legacy and longevity. Hampson cites the strong ethical backbone of the organization and a laser focus on finding the best talent that led him to being an early leader in Napa's push for gender equality among winemakers. He points out that one of Far Niente's female winemakers did not want to be seen as an outstanding female winemaker. She was an outstanding winemaker, period.

In addition to this matter-of-fact commitment to excellence, Hampson also teaches leaders that it's not enough to be good at their jobs. They also need to be teachers and coaches for others so that the people behind them will understand the why behind how decisions get made. This dedication to an "each one teach one" philosophy has allowed Far Niente's culture to be pushed as far into the organization as possible. Every person has buy-in, because everyone understands their role and value.

During your fact-finding mission in the Leaders Empathize step, you likely uncovered patterns in the experiences of people at different levels of the company. You can use your learnings to explore the best tactics to enlist your managers in the culture design journey. These people leaders have a direct connection to your frontline workers, who in consumer-facing businesses have an outsized impact on the customer experience. Anyone who has been to a fast-food restaurant with sticky floors and fries cooked in old grease knows that good management at the front makes a world of difference. But often, these managers are spread so thin doing administrative tasks, filling in for an understaffed team, and generally putting out fires that they don't have the time or energy to coach or lead the very people they are charged with managing. A store manager isn't just overseeing inventory and time sheets, they are also there to manage *people*.

From Krista's Notes App

In my twenties, I was an actress trying to make it in the big city. This meant I gained a lot of experience working in frontline jobs in hospitality, restaurants, and retail. I saw firsthand the way poor senior leadership trickled down to our managers and frontline workers. (And I made sure my father, who led one of these companies, knew my experiences!) We received directives from on high that didn't make sense with our day-to-day operations and frustrated our customers. At the same time, we were constantly told our opinions mattered. My favorite job during this time was at a high-end bakery chain where one of my suggestions was responded to—and implemented by—the CEO themself. The job also took great care in hiring, training, and promoting managers that were fully committed to the company's values, so much so that even in peak Covid lockdown, I looked forward to my 7 a.m. shifts. Many leaders think that kind of care for their front lines isn't cost-effective, but they're wrong. Turnover is expensive, and there are untold costs in customer satisfaction, too. One of the quickest ways to scuttle culture design is to not engage the front lines directly, whatever the business is.

If you start to address the needs of these managers, they will be much more willing to do what is necessary to enlist their direct reports in your culture design. Freed-up time and energy will create more trust between middle and more senior managers, which can increase both the enthusiasm for and ability to help cascade your change agenda. Why would they do more than tick the boxes if you don't demonstrate that you have been listening to their questions, concerns, and, most important, their ideas? Many seasoned managers have become jaded by the rigmarole of corporate coming in with big talk and little action. They see potential solutions to challenges and innovations that could help the business but are ignored by HQ. You're going to need to put your money where your mouth is to win over these powerful allies. Trust must be built at all levels and across functional areas.

You can start by addressing the needs that will help them succeed. Leaders can give frontline managers:

- *An ear.* Listen to their ideas and take them seriously.

- *Time.* Give them the space to train and extend the culture.

- *The right tech.* Use digital tools that make their jobs easier rather than bloat bureaucracy. Maybe you can cut a subscription for a project management tool nobody uses, while adding an AI transcription tool to make weekly standups more efficient.

One major need of middle managers is harnessing technology to better enable them to focus on what matters most. Many workers, from grant writers to illustrators to cashiers, are worried they will be automated out of a job. This fear is not new—it goes back to the industrial revolution—but it is a relevant concern in an age of rapid automation through AI and machine learning. It would be disingenuous to say all jobs will remain the same; many people will need to be reskilled. Many jobs will be transformed or eliminated completely. But the proliferation of these tools should have the potential to bring out what's best about being human by automating, streamlining, or eliminating "robotic" tasks. Don't you feel so much more "you" meeting with clients or leading a product team than trying to get the design elements of your slide deck centered?

For technology to be used in a way that enables us to be more ourselves, we must once again come back to purpose and values. What are the tasks that are better done by a person? Are your chatbots reducing friction or just leaving you with reduced costs but frustrated customers? Is your AI-generated copy worth the cost savings from cutting a talented copywriter? Cost-versus-value decisions are tricky to balance, but purpose must be a factor along with the bottom line. Focusing solely on reducing costs often costs *more* in the long run. (Just look to the human, environmental, and consumer costs of fast fashion for a stark example.) The culture design payoff of harnessing technology thoughtfully is multifaceted. When managers see that you are committed to addressing their needs, they will be more likely to work with you on implementing new technologies, rather than resisting them or finding workarounds—which is what so often happens with digital transformations. Additionally, the efficiency and human-centric nature of these thought processes doubles down on the behaviors needed for modern, thoughtfully designed cultures.

We must invest in middle managers with the right training, tools, clear priorities, and growth opportunities. This means ensuring they are fully trained in the behaviors you want to ingrain throughout the organization, so they can in turn confidently train their direct reports. If you don't train or reskill high-potential managers, you're going to lose out on great talent. Training as it applies to culture design is much more expansive than "teach them the new set of values." If you want people to *live* the values, they also need the tools (be it leadership training or a technical boot camp to upskill them) that will enable them to succeed in the role you've taken so much time to define. It's clear that across industries, but especially in the restaurant and retail space, the way we work cannot remain the same.

One retailer we work with pressure-tested its culture design through what was essentially a listening tour in different markets. This allowed the CEO to get on the ground with middle managers and gauge frontline responses to her strategy. This CEO started by refining her long-term vision with her executive team, as you did in the Leaders Define the Reality step. They distilled which messages should be workshopped and further refined as she visited retail operations across the country, meeting with general managers and teams at the store and multiunit level. As part of her iterative process, she captured the responses and integrated them into her feedback loop to drive buy-in to the change initiatives and improve the execution in real time. The hallmark of the plan was the disciplined engagement across each geographic region of the company and the meticulous messaging back into the organization. Through communication, intentional iteration, and meticulously bringing culture to life with the buy-in of middle managers, the company was able to deliver two straight years of record sales, profit, and significant growth of locations.

Opening two-way communication mechanisms to ladder up feedback from entry-level and frontline workers goes hand and hand with partnering with middle managers. This may require a mindset shift for top leaders and the perception of lower-level employees. The common framing of many of these as "unskilled workers" contributes to the idea such employees are interchangeable and that their feedback isn't a priority. Even if you aren't thinking this consciously, you may have absorbed years of rhetoric about entry-level employees (who are indeed the heart and soul of your company). But when you switch up your language and mindset around frontline workers, you can push the culture further through the business—where the customers and clients can see it. Changing the way you think about and interact with employees who are lower on the corporate ladder closes the loop on your purpose, which usually looks like "to do [. . .] for [X customer/client/member], etc." Middle managers connect you to that missing link to the people you are ultimately serving. Your culture design is there to create great companies that best serve your customers. Great companies are great places to work for all employees so that they can show up for all stakeholders.

Much like those often-disregarded frontline workers, the empathy the Bay Club CEO Matthew Stevens has for his associates is driven by his own experience of being asked when he was going to "get a real job." He told us he is passionate about professionalizing the health, fitness, and hospitality industry. That includes shifting the conversation about what makes a career or a "real job" as well as structuring compensation for people to get paid fair wages. He said his associates being able to buy a house or put their kids through college or start their dream business is what gets him out of bed in the morning. A sign that a thoughtfully designed culture has been fully brought to life is when customers (such as the Bay Club's loyal members) start noticing.

Not everyone has the firsthand experience of working on the front lines in their industry, but everyone can find ways to better empathize with the folks who work for them. For Timothy Escamilla of Bolthouse Fresh Foods, a simple way of understanding the experiences of farm workers is by visiting their on-site restroom, which he always does. The state of these facilities is his litmus test for overall work conditions. "Because if you're not able to sit down on that seat, then how do you expect anybody else to sit down on that seat?"[4] Get familiar with the daily realties of your frontline employees so that the decisions that impact the entire company are better informed and more likely to succeed throughout the entire chain of command.

Attracting great workers is important to the vitality of your culture, but how do you get them to stay? Escamilla is a big proponent of the old school "management by walking around" method—so much so that he moved from his home in the sunny coastal town of Salinas to the agricultural landscape of Bakersfield. He believed that being near the frontline team in an agricultural business was critical to drive results and actualize cultural values like accountability and being present with one another. This kind of proximity humanizes you, too. A leader who is seen often will likely receive more honest communication than the elusive "big boss" who might as well be a mythical figure. If the pandemic taught us anything, it's how much value there is in connecting in the 3D world.

Repetition, rigor, and discipline also provide the scaffolding necessary for a fully activated culture. Advantage Solutions CEO Dave Peacock uses performance reviews as a mechanism to realize his ambitions for the culture, essentially tying 50 percent of bonuses to an assessment around behaviors. The professional services firm has such enormous reach through its enterprise clients that it ends up having a hand in creating and selling products that are in "every single person's home in our country," Peacock emphasized.[5] He always wants his team to be focused on the impact they're having on the consumer. While Advantage Solutions is a B2B company providing solutions in retail sales, marketing, design, fulfillment, and more, Peacock always tells his team to "look past our clients to their consumers," because those are the people who ultimately matter most to the client.

James has worked with and for many other great leaders in the consumer products industry who have centered the needs of the consumer. One of the most influential leaders in his career was Jim Kilts, who was the CEO and chairman of Gillette when James was an executive there. One of the finest leaders James has met throughout his thirty-plus years of operational experience, Kilts was hyper-focused on what mattered most to the consumers and employees alike. He was able to bring Gillette's high-performance culture to life throughout the company via routines that were systematized in every function of the organization.

A stickler for process, Kilts implemented rigor around reporting, including a tally every morning of how many razors, batteries, and toothbrushes were sold the day before. In a 2002 interview with *Fortune*, people who had worked under Kilts noted that while his management style was demanding, they learned and grew so much under him that, years later, they still use many of the processes he instituted. James feels the same and wants readers to emulate this aspect of Kilts's leadership: meticulous attention to detail. Just as life is lived moment to moment, culture is brought to life through the tiniest details. Key details for Kilts included paying close attention to middle managers and frontline workers as well as suppliers and partners. Even before he officially took the helm, Kilts traveled with Gillette salespeople, visited stores, and inspected warehouses and manufacturing plants. According to the *Fortune* article, "during a visit to one of the company's big retail customers, a buyer told him bluntly that he always waited until the last week of the quarter to order anything from Gillette 'because I know you will always cut a deal.'" Eureka moments like these, gleaned from staying close to the ground, ultimately saved the company millions of dollars. And by modeling this disciplined, unerringly detailed style of working, he instilled values like personal responsibility and creative problem-solving throughout every level of the company. This included people in the middle and on the front lines, like salespeople on the road, who, armed with more realistic and specific targets for their quarterly performance, stopped cutting bad end-of-quarter deals out of desperation.

The work ethic brought to life by Kilts's leadership was one of measured, sustainable growth. And each member of the team who embodied those values brought to life one of the most dramatic turnarounds in the consumer goods industry before Gillette was acquired by Procter & Gamble in 2005.[6]

For James, whether it was during his time at Jamba, Gillette, or Safeway, having clear processes helped keep the organizations focused on key priorities and always allowed the company to understand what mattered most during the week, month, and quarter. It also ensured that leaders could understand the tools, training, and appropriate support that middle managers needed to lead their teams and to be on the same page about what good work for each role looked like.

The team at Gillette also used feedback mechanisms on a quarterly and annual basis to ensure that there was strong alignment with the culture and the capabilities that were being built and the results to be delivered. These mechanisms were both quantitative and qualitative to ensure executional excellence. The feedback happened at the company level, within departments and functions, and one-on-one with each leader as refinements were made.

In well-managed companies, the vitality of the culture is demonstrated by engagement of team members, satisfaction of clients, and the impact on the communities that companies live and work in. Gillette was one of the best-performing consumer products companies—fully realized culture design always shows up in the results. There was a strong tie to the cultural work that it did with its multiyear strategic plan, and it worked in what James calls an almost magical way to drive both collaboration and high performance. Throughout James's decades of experience as an executive, highly engaged teams and cultures have outperformed their competitors. Most of these companies have one foundational pillar focused on engagement, human capital, and culture built into both annual operating and three- to five-year strategic plans. In our experience with clients at Culture Design Lab, it's always a major tell to us when culture and employee engagement aren't clear strategic priorities with targeted measurement.

Another moment that stands out for James is a significant culture shift at Nestlé Purina, where he spent a large chunk of his early career. Its culture design was brought to life when the company shifted to focus more on the pet care category, where it was already a leader. This realignment involved deepening the organization's knowledge of the industry and moving out of functional siloes to improve cross-functional capabilities, which pushed a culture of transparency and collaboration deeper into the organization. One way the company formalized open communication throughout every level was through rigorous training on the skills and conditions for engagement we discussed in chapter 3. Additionally, the top leaders toured in teams of two all the factories and sales offices, addressing employees across the organization to zero in on high performance. Once again, leadership was making itself visible to people at all levels to demonstrate a commitment to center the needs of all employees. This allowed leadership teams to unlock new ways to engage with customers, whether through advertising, merchandising, or other means, and build leaders across every level of the organization.

Doing your due diligence on the changing needs of your workforce will allow you to push your culture design into every corner of your company by customizing career ladders, rewards, and recognition to increase productivity, build trust, and reduce attrition. Your middle managers enable that to happen—they are the ones who have a direct connection to the folks taking orders, selling the company rewards program, or packing products. They have a unique ability to make or break the work experience of entire teams and in turn need the support and training from senior management and above. You will know your culture is fully alive when customers and clients begin to take notice—whether it is in the form of direct feedback, social media posts, or an uptick in sales. As we evolve and adjust to the rapidly changing work life of what many are calling the Fourth Industrial Revolution, harnessing technology as a tool to unlock human progress for all will be a distinguishing factor between great companies and those that fizzle out.

Takeaways

- Middle management is critical in bringing culture to life and must be invested in.

- Middle managers must have the right training, tools, and incentives to lead their teams.

- Consider reframing your ideas about "unskilled" labor.

- All leaders at every level should spend time on the ground whenever possible to gain more insight into their employees' lives.

- Build mechanisms that reinforce and reward cultural priorities and desired behaviors.

Part Three

Measure What Matters

Chapter 6

Leaders Measure Progress

"Feedback, to me, is a gift. I want to know what's on your mind, because I want to make the best decision that's going to make this organization thrive."

—Former Kaiser Permanente CEO Bernard Tyson

We are through two parts of the culture design process. You've done your archaeological dig, using empathy to understand worker and customer experiences. You've identified the gaps between those lived experiences and your company values. You've also imagined the culture as you hope it exists in the future through your intervention and design. You've taken your first steps to implementing the culture through communication, new policies, new technology, and more. You've iterated on these new features of the culture, adjusting and adapting as you saw the culture develop, just like you'd iterate on a new product. And you've made sure, especially as the organization scaled, that the culture permeated all levels and was brought to life for all stakeholders.

We're not done yet. It's time to measure your culture design's effectiveness. Measuring the health of your culture is one of the hardest aspects of culture design to wrap your mind around. It's also one of the most important—just like monitoring your cholesterol or blood sugar informs your health-care decisions and exposes potential problems (or opportunities) that would otherwise remain hidden.

Both the quantitative and qualitative measures of your culture enable you to take the right actions to support the vitality of your organization. You must measure your results so that you can have hard data to confirm the daily feedback you've gleaned about what is working and what needs to be adjusted. To go back to the health-care metaphor, measurement is preventative care for your culture design. You may be doing all the right things with the extensive systems and behavior changes you've already cascaded throughout the organization. Measurement provides extra assurance that you're moving in the right direction, while exposing potential blind spots. It is also a key element of documentation for future leaders and your stakeholders—like investors—who want to understand how all this culture work is really panning out and why how the investment is paying off.

This chapter is about measuring progress and identifying opportunities and gaps as you shape, shift, or transform your culture. At Culture Design Lab, we view measurement as a virtuous cycle. Across James's thirty-plus years as an operating executive and board member, he's recognized that at the best-performing companies, feedback, measurement, and listening systems are always well designed and maintained. While some of these systems are formalized, many of the most useful ways leaders gather in real time input to improve culture are informal or unconventional.

Just by going through the process you have at this point means that you already have a ton of data, and you should use the tools and examples that follow to refine what you'd like to measure, how often you'd like to evaluate the results, and what methods you'd like to use to analyze it. You'll also need to come up with some systems to decide how and when to make potential adjustments in priority areas. Some of the prioritization tools we discussed earlier will come in handy here. Depending on where you are in your documentation process, the following tools can be useful as you fine-tune your measurement procedures. If you get this right, you'll be setting up your future self—and the leaders who come after you—for greater continued success with your culture design.

Choose What to Measure

It's important to understand that you can't directly measure culture at all. What you can do is develop an understanding of which behaviors, attitudes, and employee demographic data have the strongest impact on your culture. Leaders use data to iterate, and that includes how you measure the data itself. If that sounds a little meta, think back to your high school chemistry class. If you've ever created a lab report, you may remember the methodology section. The *how* has a huge impact on the results and conclusions of experiments. Things like having too small a sample size, asking leading questions, or failing to measure key data can result in incomplete, skewed, or inconclusive findings. Refining your methodology over time is what it takes to go from classroom science experiment to peer-reviewed research. (We're compressing years of intensive study, but you get the picture.)

While you will want to be thoughtful with your choices of what to measure, always keep in mind that your formal enterprise-wide surveys are not somehow the data you should solely rely on, especially if you include bespoke surveys in your data collection repertoire. You can reevaluate and tweak the data you collect annually, quarterly, or even monthly for your smaller-scale pulse surveys.

But how do you choose what initial data to collect and how to collect it? And how often should you be checking the score? Well, it depends. The timescale affects what you measure. Some information—like attrition or hiring stats—will necessarily be collected on a rolling basis, even if it is only reviewed periodically. Other data, like your annual in-depth engagement survey, will be collected only once a year. There are smaller formal and informal check-ins that fall somewhere in between.

David Satterwhite, the CEO of employee mentorship platform Chronus, has strong opinions about what to measure (retention and regrettable churn rates and employee net promoter scores [eNPS]) and why (to track employee engagement and performance). He has always been meticulously focused on culture and fixing the employee engagement gap throughout his decades as a leader. He told us that a commitment to both high performance and living the company's values exponentially increases employee engagement. From day one at Chronus, he was clear about this balance. "I will hold you just as accountable for being a great teammate and being a net positive employee to everyone around you as I will being a great performer." He has even fired top performers at various organizations who haven't been team players or values-aligned. Within his first six months at Chronus, his dedicated, balanced approach to performance and teamwork paid off as the company's eNPS shot up from around 12 (fair to average) to the 50s (excellent). This is just one way the company has been able to track the ROI of its commitment to culture design, but Satterwhite stressed that it is one of the most important. There's no way that there won't be a return on a more engaged workforce, and he wanted to remind leaders, "Any single human being can give you 20 percent output or 120 percent output; the choice is yours on how you engage and focus."[1]

The way you choose your key metrics will include some combination of measures related to your unique goals and company purpose (such as custom ratings and open-ended questions on specific initiatives) as well as standard culture measures that will be relevant for most companies. Some of these include:

- Engagement scores such as net referrer scores, attrition and turnover rates, and ratings around belonging, well-being, and satisfaction

- Overall demographic data including race/ethnic background, gender, LGBTQIA+ identity, veteran status, disability, etc.

- Hiring and promotion data filtered by the metrics above as well as the rates of internal versus external recruitment to provide insight into your talent pipeline and the development of your bench

For a sense of what your industry peers are measuring and how your numbers relate to theirs, you can use tools like employee engagement software Culture Amp's comprehensive benchmarking data, broken out by industry and region. Their engagement surveys include dozens of statements, the core five of which are:

- I would recommend [Company] as a great place to work.

- [Company] motivates me to go beyond what I would in a similar role elsewhere.

- I am proud to work for [Company].

- I rarely think about looking for a job at another company.

- I see myself still working at [Company] in two years' time.[2]

Additionally, client and consumer satisfaction surveys can provide a different, potentially more brutally honest perspective on team cohesion, innovation, and efficiency. One of the issues employers sometimes face with internal engagement surveys is that some respondents will sugarcoat their answers. This could be motivated by many factors, with generosity toward a well-liked manager on one end and fear of potential backlash for a poor review on the other. This may be especially true on small teams where an individual may worry their responses, though anonymous, will still make them easily identifiable. The people paying you for products and services, however, have no such qualms.

Since you can't measure everything, we recommend starting with the basics and focusing on long-term measures that you would review in an annual engagement survey, including the employee demographic data outlined above. Then pick three to five areas that are important both for your organization and your peers and measure yourself against industry benchmarks. You'll also want to make sure you are asking questions that evaluate the most pertinent aspects of your culture design, like having people rate the effectiveness of a new training program or including an open-ended question on how respondents would describe the culture as it stands.

Ways to Collect Data

You may be happy with your current engagement measurement tools, but if you feel it's time to reevaluate, there is a wide variety of different options from the low-tech to the comprehensive. You'll likely end up using a few tools that rotate based on timescale and the type of data collected.

Comprehensive tools

The Gallup Q12 is the gold standard for collecting employee engagement data that most of you will be familiar with. The Q12, a series of questions that build on each other to form a pyramid of engagement and growth, have been used and refined over the past twenty-five-plus years. Many of the leaders we've worked with, including James himself, have used the Q12 or a variation of it to track their progress on culture design.

Other comprehensive tools and dashboards include Culture Amp's technology (where the aforementioned benchmark data stems from) and surveys from Great Places to Work. The latter's tool is based around a five-part trust model, which is as follows:

- *Credibility:* Measures whether employees see management as credible (believable, trustworthy); assesses employees' perceptions of management's communication practices, competence, and integrity

- *Respect:* Measures whether employees feel respected by management; assesses employees' perceptions of professional support, collaboration, and involvement in decisions and the level of care management shows for employees as people

- *Fairness:* Measures whether employees believe management practices and policies are fair; assesses the equity, impartiality, and justice employees experience in the workplace

- *Pride:* Measures how employees feel about their own impact through their work, their pride in the work of their team, and their pride in the company overall

- *Camaraderie:* Measures whether employees believe their company is a strong community where colleagues are friendly, supportive, and welcoming[3]

We have been impressed by Great Places to Work for its decades of research, long-standing role as an authority in what makes a workplace outstanding, and in the past few years, the addition of "For All" to its mission. What may seem like a small addendum amounts to a renewed focus on inclusion that we see as fundamental to modern, sustainable leadership. To be a For All leader requires you to focus on both the team as a whole and on the individuals and cross-sections that make up your workforce.

Self-evaluation frameworks

Methods that lean more toward self-evaluation than evaluating the organization at large give leaders a snapshot over time of how effective their culture design has been from an individual accountability perspective.

📝 From Krista's Notes App

As the co-managing editor for the twenty-first volume of *Lumina*, the Sarah Lawrence graduate literary magazine, I created and iterated on several mechanisms for feedback and self-evaluation. Managing a team of thirty and whittling down hundreds of submissions to a few dozen to create a cohesive journal (a designed culture for the edition, if you will) required significant levels of organization. I learned so much about myself as a leader—I love a good automatic process, and things worked most smoothly with my team when we overcommunicated. Keeping track of everything in the form of diligent notes, spreadsheets, and meeting recap emails helped me keep track of where my communications were working and the places where I could use some more clarity in my systems. Not every leader will have the same loves and predilections as I do, but the act of being aware of the ones that resonate with you, and then collecting data on how they affect the culture design, will help the process.

In this respect, one tried-and-true framework for leaders is the Organizational Culture Assessment Instrument (OCAI). Like the Gallup Q12, the OCAI has been around for decades and is used to evaluate your culture through a matrix. It can be a good tool to use in concert with the data that is focused on team engagement and feedback. This matrix framework means that there is no objective benchmark to strive for; rather, it can give you a sense of the positionality of your culture based on four general culture types:

- *Clan.* Clan (or "collaborate culture") creates a sense of a close-knit family in the workplace. The organization is held together by loyalty and tradition. Promotes teamwork, participation, and consensus.

- *Adhocracy.* Adhocracy (or "create culture") places an emphasis on giving employees the space to think outside of the box and allowing them to take risks with the goal of innovation.

- *Market.* Market (or "compete culture") places profitability above all else. A results-based workplace that emphasizes targets, deadlines, and getting things done. People are competitive and focused on goals.

- *Hierarchy.* Hierarchy (or "control culture") operates through a vertical management structure with strict control. Procedures direct what people do. Leaders are proud of efficiency-based coordination and organization. Keeping the organization functioning smoothly is most crucial.[4]

Among these four, you may decide to strive for one or a particular mix based on your goals, industry, and current standing.

As we learned from Chief Executives for Corporate Purpose (CECP) Daryl Brewster, the organization has great annual review and quarterly check-in templates that they use with their clients. These are also incremental tools for self-evaluation. They are geared toward CEOs and executives but can be applied to other roles and functions. The questions focus on results and upcoming goals as they relate to both overall professional development and CECP's values. These values (influence; innovation; diversity, equity, and inclusion; and authentic action) are useful starting points for most companies, to tweak and refine as they see fit. This kind of self-reflection adds color to the full picture of your leadership and creates ritual and documentation for yourself, ensuring you remain on track as the visionary steward of your culture design.

Low-tech but effective

Not all useful measurement tools are from major survey companies and backed by a robust suite of cutting-edge data analysis. If you are a small company, surveying a small cross-section of your team, or focused on a shorter time scale, don't discount the simpler solutions. Easy-to-use, pared-down, and free or inexpensive options are great for when you don't need deeply sophisticated statistical analysis. Tools like Google Forms or Survey Monkey have a very low barrier to entry for survey makers and respondents alike. Powerful dashboards are great in many large enterprise settings, but sometimes all you need is a good spreadsheet. Examples of times to use these types of tools include asking a few very specific questions, surveying a group of a hundred or less, or receiving responses from clients who may be less tech-savvy. Maybe you want to get a quick pulse on a situation after rolling out a new aspect of your culture design. A low-tech tool may be enough to get a feel for how it's landing.

Additionally, you can brush off your interview skills and collect feedback via one-on-one conversations, town halls, and roundtables. This strategy is typically not feasible at scale but can provide a snapshot and add dimension you may not receive in written responses. An idea you may want to steal: some employee engagement platforms have started integrating video or audio recordings into their two-way messaging capabilities. Depending on their communication and learning style, leaving a voice note may be more accessible and yield better results than typical surveys for some of your employees.

From James's Notepad

So much more gets done when you have shared mechanisms for straightforward, respectful feedback. For your team to work together at the highest level, you need to cut out as many chances for miscommunication as possible. How do you create an environment where no one is cut out of key conversations (e.g., giving important directives one-on-one that should be shared on a group level) and issues are brought up in a timely, direct, and thoughtful manner? We understand that the impulse to dance around straight feedback often comes from a good place: we don't want to make others feel bad, and we worry the feedback may do that. But there are many ways, outlined in this chapter, to be honest and forthright without being disrespectful. There's a line here between candor and tactlessness, and you can learn to stay on the right side.

Customized and qualitative measurement

The bulk of your measurement will create hard data like ratings and demographic numbers, but collecting qualitative data through open-ended survey questions and feedback mechanisms provides additional context and detail that further clarify the quantitative data. We were inspired by marketing and communications expert Tony Wells's description of the say/do gap, which is a great way to conceptualize the space between words and actions as a measurement of how effectively your culture design has been brought to life. Your goal will always be to narrow the gap between vision and reality, and we can imagine using say/do as a framework for both self-reflective evaluation and survey questions. In surveys, it could work on multiple levels. You should add questions that garner responses to the following: To what extent do your employees feel that you've successfully accomplished what you said you would? And how aware are they of your vision in the first place?

Google's Sam Bright closes the loop on qualitative data by framing his follow-ups as "You said . . . /We did . . . /What's next?" After his leadership team analyzes engagement surveys, Bright compiles responses from them that he will in turn share with the team at large. An email is sent out with sections from each senior leader reading something like the following: "You [the team as a whole] said X in Y question from the engagement survey. We did Z in response to your [the team as a whole] feedback. What's next for the leadership is to continue acting on the team's feedback by XYZ." This method of internal communication allows him to ensure the team at large understands that their voices matter and are being integrated into the overall strategy. These feedback loops are critical to sustaining a healthy culture.

Crystallize Your Findings

Now that you're armed with a dossier full of measurements, you must find a way to analyze and distill them in a clear, digestible fashion. Even if you have great data analysts on your team, you'll want to have a broad understanding of the raw data as well as an idea of what you'd like to highlight.

When you're looking at your results, you'll want to pull out key themes. Create a single view with simple declaratives on the following kinds of big-picture topics:

- Where are you doing well overall?

- Where are the opportunities for growth?

- Which data points are stable (for measures you have previous scores for)?

As you dig into the measurements, you'll want to look for significant gaps based on demographics by disaggregating the data. This includes looking at segments based on identity (race, gender, disability, etc.), function or business unit, and level. For example, look at how a question like "I plan to be at [Company] in two years' time" elicits different answers from senior leaders versus middle managers. To push it further, you should look at key cross-sections. For example, do women of color overall have comparable employee satisfaction scores to men of color, white men, or white women? Do female senior leaders have different experiences than male senior leaders? And so on. Cross-sectional data creates endless possibilities of combinations (e.g., "What's the satisfaction level of female frontline employees between the ages of twenty-six and thirty in region A versus region B?"). You don't want to get too fine with this at first. We recommend focusing on a few high-impact cross-sections, likely areas that came up in the beginning of your culture design process. Dig into polarizing topics (say, a nearly 50/50 split in favorability on an employee satisfaction question). You can look at whether there are patterns and what direction they're trending in.

Present your findings to the entire company (in the case of a year-end engagement survey or similar) and conduct team-level meetings for each manager to debrief with their respective teams, paying particular attention to any places where the team data may deviate (for better or worse) from the company averages. Drive home the point that your ambition, vision, or purpose by saying, "Your culture design is X, and the data indicates that the organization (or Y team/unit) is at Z point in bringing X to life. To address this progress/gap, we will continue accelerating or adjust the integration of our culture design by doing XYZ." With any questions you've asked previously in either the same or a comparable configuration, you have the benefit of comparison to give your perspective. If you are a younger organization or have questions that are new or significantly transformed, you should be able to look at industry benchmark data to get a general idea of what you should be aiming for.

Data visualization is a fantastic tool for mapping culture to measurements (just ask our editor, Scott, who literally wrote the book on it!). Visualization is excellent for distilling the big-picture stage by showing clear, simple representations of the key measures you're watching. It's useful in your visualizations of the measurements to

FIGURE 6-1

Good data visualization helps measure what matters

In an intentionally designed culture, good visualization will help measure what matters with transparency. The example on the left suffers from clutter and exaggerates the positive trend. It also lacks any "virtue lines," the benchmarks you are striving to reach. The example on the right presents the same data in a way that is clearer, less exaggerated, and more actionable.

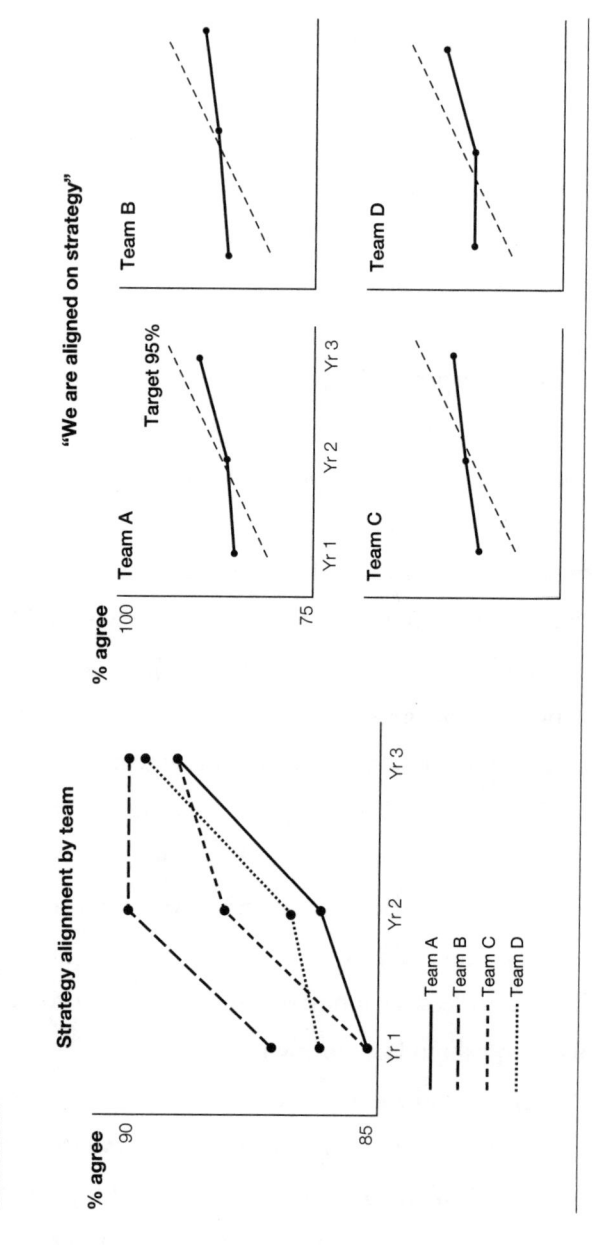

Strategy alignment by team

"We are aligned on strategy"

include what Scott calls "virtue marks"—targets and goals you're trying to reach (and conversely, levels and floors you want to stay above) to see if you're ahead or behind on hitting the target numbers. Just ensure that you're making visualizations with simplicity, contextualization, and transparency in mind, lest you end up with more confusion than clarity. For example, you'll want to avoid scales that exaggerate or downplay results, and you want to avoid trying to cram many measures into one or two charts. Let each chart express one measure, one idea. See figure 6-1.

If you're working with a large dataset that includes a significant number of open-ended questions, you can ask your data or machine learning team to use language processing tools like sentiment analysis to identify patterns. These can also be used (with great care for privacy) to analyze other types of text, such as public posts and comments on your company's intranet, or even scraped data about your organization from social media and forums. Depending on your needs and capabilities, there are many out-of-the-box AI solutions that summarize and pull key themes out of text. One we love for meetings and interviews is Otter.ai, one of the more accurate transcription tools we've found. Many comprehensive survey platforms also have built-in functionality for analyzing open-ended responses.

Take Action

Doing something with your findings is the most important part of the measurement process. Executive coach, author, and consulting firm GlobalEdg founder Paul Butler uses certain levers, mentioned briefly in chapter 2, that are helpful in determining how to move the needle on your focus areas. You can't work on everything at once; consider prioritizing a combination of areas where you can have the most impact and places where you foresee quick wins that will keep the team motivated. From his years of experience in strategy and leadership, Butler has zeroed in on cultural levers that, when pulled, are effective in driving internal and external results. At the individual level, these include:

- Leadership

  - This lever is around your mission, purpose, values, and action plan. At this stage, you're already working this lever regularly and would pull it if employee feedback on management (or your own self-evaluations) reveals significant issues around leaders' effectiveness.

- Capabilities

  - Capabilities in this context refer to opportunities for growth, training, and development, as well as refining your hiring, recruitment, and succession planning systems. You'd pull this lever if engagement data reveals dissatisfaction or doubt around employees' futures at the company. It is also an important lever to pull when there are experience gaps based on demographics or if you find there are backgrounds that are significantly underrepresented.

- Behaviors

  - These include clearly defining roles and tasks and ensuring that every person understands—in the words of Timothy Escamilla—"what a good day looks like."[5]

  - Leaders should work to integrate culture by taking daily actions.

- Identify the underlying beliefs and assumptions that have been shaping behaviors.

- These levers can be pulled when people don't understand the connection between your culture design and their daily lived reality or when they lack clarity on their purpose within the organization.

At the organization level, Butler's levers comprise:

- Structure

  - The constraints, systems, and guidelines within which work gets done. Examples include HR processes, paths to advancement, and your org chart.

  - Physical structure—the buildings or dispersed physical spaces that constitute the workplace play a big role in productivity. Optimizing them depends on your industry and company purpose as well as role and function. The physical workspace will come into play if you've asked a question about remote, hybrid, or fully in-person work and people are dissatisfied with the status quo.

  - As with individual capabilities, use these levers when the data reveals uncertainty about peoples' futures at the company and lack of clarity around their roles.

- Policies and processes

  - Formal policies and processes that govern all employees' rights, freedoms, and constraints—in other words, what you encourage and what you will not tolerate.

- This lever is strongly linked to alarm bells raised around psychological safety, inclusion, and belonging.

- Rewards and recognition

  - Compensation systems including overall pay, benefits, and bonuses.

  - Recognition, whether done at smaller intervals or larger opportunities annually and at particular milestones.

  - Pull this lever if there is a gap revealed in whether people feel appropriately compensated for the work they do, or in response to a question of whether their work matters or is meaningful.

- Information

  - Company and teamwide communication systems.

  - Symbols and shared language.[6]

  - You'd pull this if surveys reveal a lack of clarity around transparency and two-way communication.

Butler's levers serve as useful tools for you to assess and prioritize where you can make the most positive change quickest based on your measurements and which areas expose the biggest needs. We also encourage you to take a collaborative approach to your action plan, as you have throughout this culture design process. See how you can find a way to engage people across functions and levels. Say, "It looks like we're not where we want to be on rewards and recognition, so I'm going to put together a cross-functional team with members from every level of the org to work on that." You should also find ways to integrate these actions as adjustments to your ongoing systems and rituals. The cyclical nature of the culture design process is intended to be integrative, not an overhaul. You're not tearing one thing out and putting another thing in. You're slowly mixing in new culture elements and replacing or taking out old ones. Your response to the data should be supplemental and additive; no need to create extra work unnecessarily.

Make inspiration part of your plan because your people will feel the weight of change. Sometimes they may feel like they're making no progress. Inspire your team by keeping your sights on the long-term vision, reminding people that you are confident it will pay off, and citing places in which it already has as evidence. Advantage Solutions CEO Dave Peacock told us the North Star that keeps him on track with culture design is the ambition to be on the *Fortune* and Great Places to Work annual list of the top hundred companies to work for. "If we achieve that, I feel like it is a signal that people feel like they belong . . . that they feel their whole person is embraced—not just accepted, but embraced—by the organization and that they understand their role."[7] You likely have your own version of this ambition. Don't let it out of your sight.

Once you've nailed down how you are going to respond to your survey findings, use the communication systems you've fine-tuned to ensure that everyone knows where you're going and that you are taking their responses seriously. We learned long ago in math class to show our work; the same principle applies here too.

A Note on Survey Fatigue

One issue that may be on your mind when reading about regular check-ins is the danger of too many surveys and too much feedback.

Nobody wants to be micromanaged, and in a world where we are inundated by Slack messages, emails, and incoming tasks, it is important to be mindful about all the asks you're making. One thing to remember about survey fatigue is that it is exacerbated by ensuing inaction. If employees repeatedly take the time to provide feedback and then see no demonstrable change or follow-up, they are far less inclined to want to continue providing it. Your trust-building work will be key to increasing your people's response level. Additionally, you need to be willing to adjust your asks as necessary, such as reducing the number of pulse surveys during your busiest season. Providing context is important both when seeking feedback and in the contents of your questions to the team. Tailoring your questionnaires to your organization as well as to the relevant topic or team makes the process feel more thoughtful. Open-ended questions are great; they provide rich texture and can be mined for nuanced sentiments. Still, use them only for the most crucial areas you want that detailed feedback for. Too many open-ended questions make people reluctant to complete a survey or just make their answers in all those blank boxes terse. Consider scales or ratings as an alternative in some cases.

Follow up with some communication of findings as soon as you can after you conduct your survey. Even if it is as simple as "Here are our initial takeaways, and this is what we'll be doing in the coming days/weeks/months to address them" you'll create goodwill with your workers. Design thinking best practices demonstrate that it's better to make the process easy for users than it is to try to capture comprehensive feedback. For example, delivery apps like Doordash and customer service platforms like ZenDesk collect massive amounts of feedback with one click from users through automated emails or push notifications that ask you to rate your order or the customer service you received. Take a page out of their books and consider where you can gain valuable information from a simple "How are we doing on X?" These kinds of demonstrations of good faith will make people more likely to participate in future surveys.

. . .

Though this may be the end of the process we have outlined, it is only the beginning of your culture design journey. You'll likely cycle through the culture design process, making modifications as you see fit for your organization, many times. Our hope is that you will use the above measurement tools to continuously monitor your culture, remain nimble, and keep your focus on the larger goal and purpose of your company. In the next and final chapter, we'll explore what it means to be steadfast in this cyclical work and how committing to culture design will help you build your legacy.

Takeaways

- If it matters, you measure it, which also goes for the health of your culture.

- Design your surveys and other feedback mechanisms as thoughtfully as you are designing your culture.

- Include the customer and client experience as part of evaluating your organizational health.

- The best leaders are always looking for continual feedback and measurement opportunities.

- Be strategic with how you present your findings to the team.

- Put the locus of your energy on action: doing what matters is what makes measurement a virtuous cycle.

Conclusion

Leaders Build a Future That Works for All

"A society grows great when its leaders plant trees whose shade they know they shall never sit in."

—Ancient proverb

While compiling the best tools and frameworks to complement our culture design process, we had the absolute honor of speaking with many great leaders. Whether we had known them for years or had only recently met them, these leaders, so generous with their time and wisdom, shared valuable, actionable advice that we in turn have been able to share with you. Our ambition with this work is to provide guidance as you build organizations with a culture that you *shape*, not one you inherit or just let emerge. We want to help you create purposeful organizations, and make a case for investing in legacy, sustainability, and longevity.

Building a Future for All

So how does a great leader build a future for all? We believe it is a future that is chiefly concerned with ensuring equitable access to opportunity and resources. Opportunities for job growth, wealth building, and upward mobility as well as other foundational needs like clean air and water, health care, nourishing food, and shelter. Your role in meeting these needs will vary based on your purpose and industry, but don't discount this vision just because you don't think it applies to the work you do. We've worked with all kinds of companies that want to build an intentional culture and create a better future, from family-owned companies that sell jarred jalapeños to global pharmaceutical businesses. Regardless of industry, company size, location, or any other factor, you have a bigger potential role in the future than you see at first glance. Your most obvious role is your company's ability to be an equitable job creator, which has a ripple effect on growth, culture, and innovation. But you also can be an industry leader in the broad mission of improving people's lives. Whether you are a multinational energy company researching solar power or a small retail chain that organizes with their regional chambers of commerce for local causes, don't underestimate your ability to help shape a better tomorrow.

You can also foster intergenerational collaboration. The workplace today is more intergenerational than ever—soon it will be common for four generations to be sharing the workspace—and leaders have had a difficult time bridging the gap between coworkers at different ages and life stages. But each generation has a lot to learn from the others. Mentorship has traditionally been one-way, with experienced folks providing guidance to people in earlier stages of their careers.

But many of the leaders we spoke to told us how much they'd learned from their millennial and Gen Z employees and children.

Younger people tend to have a different perspective on work, inclusion, and the future. This can look like an optimism and creativity that brings fresh energy to changing the status quo. On the other hand, Gen Z and Millennials' discontent may also show up as a renewed urgency that spurs transformation and resists stagnation. Older generations may also be pleased with their smaller-scale, practical learnings from digital natives, like how to optimize their email or fully automate tedious processes. In turn, experienced employees have abundant wisdom to share, from institutional knowledge that will help daily tasks run more smoothly, to leadership skills and networking advice. Between societal changes, rapid technological advances, and the impact of the pandemic, some of your early-career coworkers may need a little extra patience and coaching in skills you see as obvious. Krista has been told that some young Gen Z adults weren't even taught proper typing technique in school! If things can change that much in a decade, it makes sense that it would take a little legwork to bridge the gap between employees who are twenty, thirty, or forty-plus years apart.

From Krista's Notes App

There are many things I have treasured about my two years in grad school. It reignited my love of learning and academic rigor. I got to stretch my creative boundaries and experiment with more genres and forms than I could have imagined. Perhaps most importantly, I made wonderful friends with brilliant writers—of all ages. I learned something from each of them.

Conclusion

There were twenty-two-year-old poets who could teach master classes both in phonics and cultivating a strong voice on social media. There were retired lawyers and stockbrokers who taught me the value of reinvention, all while making me laugh and cry with their stunning writing. Never underestimate anyone, regardless of age or work experience. Everyone has the capacity to surprise you. One of the most rewarding aspects of building an intentional culture by design—and we've seen this with clients—is when leaders enable people to truly excel at work in ways they hadn't seen. Just as my program made me a better writer, when you have an intentional culture, you unlock so much more in your workers.

This book is an exercise in intergenerational collaboration. We both jokingly argue about which one of us has taught the other more through the process. If you can find ways to formally and informally encourage intergenerational collaboration, your teams will be better for it. Some companies have instituted two-way mentorship programs, and you should incorporate skills like patience and avoiding assumptions into your leadership training. Simply approaching others in good faith would head off many conflicts before they begin.

Belonging is an aspect of employee experience that can get overlooked because of its intangibility. What does it even mean? For us, it is related to the sense of psychological safety so often measured in engagement surveys: to belong is to feel safe bringing your whole self to work. With the rise of work-life *integration* over work-life *balance*, we have begun to acknowledge the impossibility of compartmentalizing ourselves, so now we must feel like we belong in both places in the same way. As Krista has taught James, there is no more "work me" and "home me." There's just "me." When people, especially younger generations, feel they must break themselves into parts, we notice that their sense of belonging at work decreases. This is not good for business. A low sense of belonging means workers are less committed to their companies and less present in their jobs. Engagement surveys show that this is an endemic problem that leads to attrition, increased costly turnover, and decreased customer service. Belonging matters to the bottom line and is critical as we think about the significance of millennials and Gen Z in our workforce.

We saw an aspect of this trend named on social media as "quiet quitting." And no matter how much we hide pieces of our thoughts, experiences, or identity, suppressing the realities of our lives creates an invisible mental load that will impact our output. The signs may be glaring, like missed deadlines or high turnover rates. But when people can't be their full selves, companies also miss out on unique insights that they have based on their identities, backgrounds, or vantage point within the organization. Belonging may be intangible, but it certainly has a real impact on employee engagement and discretionary effort.

The idea of belonging also speaks to the broader concept of embracing and uplifting what makes us each uniquely human. Earlier we mentioned that when used intentionally, AI and automation tools can be used to emphasize the things humans do best. Our creativity, innovation, joy, pain, and anger are all fuel for the world we would like to see. Most of us spend a third or more of our waking hours at work. With your one short, miraculous life, how can you use your role as a leader to harness the humanity of the people you work with? How can you take daily action to recognize the humanity within yourself? A commitment to humanity can be used as a guiding principle in strategic decisions. One salient example of people-first or human-centered decision-making is the implementation of flexible or hybrid return-to-office policies that respect the different needs and working styles of your employees. It can look like Timothy Escamilla's stops to the bathrooms at every site visit to ensure they are serviceable. It looks like Dirk Hampson's investment in internal training and development at Far Niente. Our current business systems are in a precarious place, having for decades—and indeed, centuries—prioritized short-term profits over people. Like an artist using destructive habits to "fuel" their creativity, this way of doing business works until, all of a sudden, it doesn't. Look at Boeing's disasters or the threat of H5N1 exacerbated by profit-first farming practices. But it is people—not a few people, *all* people—who matter most. And good news for all of us in the business of long-term, sustainable growth and profits: investing in humanity is ultimately good for the bottom line, too.

. . .

At the start of this book, we took you through an exercise to get clear on your why, and how culture design would impact you and your team. Now, we encourage you to use the slightly adjusted exercise below to dream a little bigger and expand outward. We might call this the "Know Why You Keep Going" exercise.

> I want to continue integrating a thoughtfully designed culture throughout my organization in order to _____
> _____. The impact this will have on me, my team, and the future for all is _____
> _____.

Keep It Going

Even if you can envision it, creating the conditions necessary to build a future for all is neither easy nor quick. It takes ongoing, intentional reinforcement, measurement, and integration into the organization. Depending on your ambitions and capabilities, it takes work not only within your company but also throughout your industry and the communities you serve. How do you keep the faith in the face of life's challenges, whether unprecedented or mundane? And how can your culture design survive leadership changes, mergers and acquisitions, economic headwinds and all the things that tug us away from the hard work of culture design and future design?

One way to shore up the longevity of your culture is to consistently build leaders behind you while encouraging them to do the same. Instilling this habit kicks off a chain reaction and becomes self-sustaining after the initial legwork. It reminds us of a branch of folklore called childlore, which constitutes the stories and games that are taught by children to other children. There's something to be gleaned from the way generations of children, including in the pre-internet era, have managed to learn the same games and urban legends across disparate social strata and geographies. It may seem silly to say, but there are few greater examples of institutional knowledge than a big kid teaching a little kid to play patty-cake. In the corporate context of our adult world, one way to formalize the continuous development of leaders is through mechanisms that underscore each team member's big-picture role within the company. Dirk Hampson did this at Far Niente by creating a cross-functional group with representation from each of their wineries. This group met regularly and split into small three- to four-person teams to work on relevant issues in the business, his version of an action-learning team. In this way, Hampson opened lines of communication, broke down siloes, and strengthened the organization's capability to collaborate and solve complex problems.[1]

Celebrating small wins and major milestones alike also helps sustain long-term work. Recognition can be as simple as implementing a regular round of team shout-outs, like Peace Coffee does at all-staff meetings, and as significant as Far Niente's twenty-years-of-service gift of a high-end watch. Creating celebratory rituals is also another way to center humanity, as we are hardwired to respond well to positive reinforcement. In your personal achievements, you may have learned that stopping to acknowledge how far you've come keeps you more motivated than when you simply plow through to the next goal. In a corporate context, the key is public, shared acknowledgment. Private, personal tokens like a restaurant gift card have their place in your reward system, but a group dinner may be more effective at creating momentum around successes. These celebrations do not need to be expensive or time-consuming. You can carve out a little space to shout out a team or an individual at in-person or virtual meetings or through a highlight in a companywide email. A great twist on the usual work happy hours is inventing more purpose-driven team-bonding activities like a company volunteer day of service. You can also find fun events that connect to something you've been working on—Carla Vernón brought her Pixar check-in avatars to life by taking her team at Honest to a showing of the movie *Inside Out 2*. Professional development opportunities are also a great avenue for celebration. While many people focus on big milestones like promotions and raises, smaller-scale rewards could be the opportunity to take part in a stretch project or make a presentation to the senior leadership team. Other ideas include public-facing social media shout-outs and acknowledging personal milestones as appropriate. An addition to the customary birthday cake may be a gift basket from the team for a new baby or a coworker celebrating their recently conferred PhD. As always, we encourage you to get creative, consider the simplest ways to make an impact, and tailor your celebrations to your company and team.

As a complement to celebrating small wins, continuing to develop your storytelling skills is another way to keep everyone focused on the big picture. Stories are the language of culture within and outside of business. Humans have been telling stories for longer than we've had written language. A skilled storyteller can reach beyond the corporate lingo of a company's ambitions and vision to connect their teammates with a greater collective purpose. This includes having a clear grasp on how your background has shaped you as a leader, which will serve as the foundation for how you relate to your colleagues. Narrative is a tool for connection that can do heavy lifting when it comes to ingraining culture. Remember the classic wisdom: "They won't remember what you said . . . but they'll remember how you made them feel." (Ironically, this quote itself is often misattributed to leaders including Maya Angelou, which seems to prove the point.)

Finally, you may also want to keep people motivated with visual reminders. From posters or plaques in your physical workspace to custom Zoom backgrounds, it's great to have little cues to keep on keeping on. These strategies can energize you and your team when the going gets tough and will help sustain your continued investment in culture design.

Conclusion

A Lineage of Great Leaders

The leaders we have worked with have a commitment to developing leaders behind them, but they also have role models that enabled them to be the leaders they are today. Here are a few of the learnings from inspirational leaders that our interviewees have integrated into their work.

First, there are the larger-than-life leaders, public figures who have inspired millions. The words of powerful orators, like "I never forget that I live in a house owned by all the American people and that I have been given their trust" from FDR's 1938 fireside chat, inspire Dave Peacock to focus on a vision greater than himself. We've mentioned the way Steve Jobs's "Think different" speech encouraged Matthew Stevens to approach the fitness and hospitality industry with a Silicon Valley–inspired spirit of innovative and category-building leadership. We've had our own faith and courage bolstered by Barack Obama's use of "Yes We Can," which ushered in an era we are grateful that our parents and grandparents, sons and daughters of the Jim Crow South, were alive to witness.

Then there are the business leaders who have mentored and inspired leaders as their careers progressed. You have Dirk Hampson, whose four-decade winemaking career was accelerated by the shrewd and fiercely purpose-driven leadership style of Far Niente founder Gil Nickel. There are people like former Gillette CEO Jim Kilts, who has served as a model for how James thinks about intentionality, and former Nestlé Purina president Terry Block, whose work at that organization was a testament to how a disciplined approach to driving culture ultimately leads to high performance.

And there are a whole host of mothers, fathers, grandparents, and kin. Timothy Escamilla learned about hard work from his parents and grandfather, who started as farmworkers. Escamilla later went on to become president of Dole Fresh Foods—the modern iteration of the company where his father once worked as a lettuce packer. Talk about legacy. Dave Peacock also learned about hard work and agility from his parents, and his mother in particular, who at various times throughout his childhood worked as real estate broker, a teacher, a graphic designer, and a paralegal. This instilled in him a great reverence for the often-overlooked work women do, both within and outside of their homes. Carla Vernón credits her father, a Black Panamanian immigrant, and her mother, a Black American from segregated New Orleans, with instilling in her possibility, problem-solving, and the courage to break the mold. Growing up watching her parents' STEM careers (a field where Black folks were underrepresented—Vernón's mother was one of NASA's many "hidden figures") and Vernón's relationship to her rich Afro-Latina identity, the Honest Company's CEO has always celebrated what she calls a "gumbo" of influences and ideas in herself and others. James gets his drive and desire to be active from his dad, who only retired as a skycap at the St. Louis airport in his late eighties, due to the pandemic. And from his beloved late mother, James learned compassion, determination, and the impact it has when someone believes in you.

From James's Notepad

I can't overstate the role my parents played in making me the man I am today. They instilled in me perseverance, the value of reading and education, and the importance of finding humor and joy through life's hardships. Stop to smell the roses. My mother, Rose Marie White, passed in 2024 after a valiant battle with cancer. We dedicated this book to her, and I'll never forget how she championed me, fighting for my right to get a good education after I fell through the cracks of our school system and was put in a remedial class in fifth grade. My father, my namesake, James White, is a spitfire in his early nineties who still surprises me with his wit, his determination, his quiet confidence. I owe much to them and their legacy thrives in me and my girls. Reflect on the people who've been influential to you and how the values and traits they imbued in you can help you persevere in your effort to create a culture by design.

Krista gets to benefit from this incredible lineage, including her extremely hardworking, kind, and loving dad; her empathetic, funny, mother, a fellow writer; and her three grandparents both on Earth and passed on whom she hopes to make proud.

Who is in your leadership lineage? If they are still with us, now may be a good time to thank them.

A Final Culture Story from the Field: Schnuck Markets

In 1939, Anna Schnuck started a small corner confectionary in north St. Louis, Missouri. A shining example of a leadership lineage, Schnuck Markets is still family-owned and -operated and has grown to 115 stores throughout the Midwest. Schnucks is a familiar brand in James's hometown of St. Louis, and he has been grateful that his position on the board has given him more excuses to spend time with his family there. He's also been impressed with the vision evident in Schnucks' leadership. The company has been in business for eighty-five years, and third-generation CEO Todd Schnuck is looking ahead to year 100. Since he took the helm a decade ago, and particularly in the last several years, Schnuck has put a renewed attention on the company's mission to nourish people's lives. As he did research on the company at the start of his tenure, he came across a striking line from his father's 1991 obituary: "Don Schnuck did more than feed people. He nourished the community."[2] This inspired him to carry on this legacy and codify nourishing people's lives as the company's true north. While this has been its stated focus for years, it is only recently that there has been an energy throughout the company of truly living this value. Todd Schnuck knew from the outset that this realignment would be a long-term project. His advisory board told him, "You're just going to have to keep talking about this and talking about this and talking about this before it finally resonates."[3] He followed their advice, remaining dedicated to nourishing the lives of his employees, customers, and communities. It has paid off, with team members and the public alike taking notice of his efforts to build an intentional, beautiful culture by design.

The work the team has done of late has emphasized and nurtured what was always present. The company's solid foundations are exemplified by the long tenures of its employees, including VP of Retail Operations Stacy Brandt, who started working at a Schnucks store twenty-seven years ago. While Brandt originally thought of her position as simply a part-time job to help pay for school, she quickly realized she could build a career for herself at Schnucks. The roles she had as she took on wider responsibilities through the years gave her the opportunity to connect with people every day and explore many different aspects of the business. Brandt made the point that Schnucks is not only a family business but also a business of families. Case in point: she met her husband while they were both working at Schnucks.

During our interview, Brandt and Schnuck talked to us about the impact of the work they've been doing with the Center for Intentional Leadership, facilitated by Mike Whitehead, the firm's founder. They've implemented new feedback mechanisms to drive culture and performance. One is the live 360, a process in which each key leader on the executive team receives live cross-functional feedback from their peers to increase their awareness of how their strengths and weaknesses are perceived by colleagues, and to accelerate the agility of decision making and collaboration. The other is their sports-inspired "Game Film" review, used to appraise the implementation of big projects like building a store or launching a new product or marketing campaign. A force multiplier for the culture design they've already done, the work around intentional leadership has three central pillars: be present, be relational, and be at cause. As we are faced with a constant stream of distractions, it has never been more difficult or more important to practice remaining present. Schnuck and Brandt both have plaques on their desks reading "Be here now," a reminder to fully commit to their work and teammates. The words appear around the office and living this value has made a difference, with one employee even putting up a "Be here now" sign on his back door at home to remind him to be present with his family. Schnuck told us, "People have commented about how it's had an impact on their entire life and that goes back to nourishing people's lives."[4]

Being relational is about trust, communication, and finding common ground. It's the trust and empathy Schnucks has fostered that has allowed for compassionate candor, thus creating a virtuous cycle. This tenet reinforces what most of us already know: that relationships are the foundation of successful businesses. And being at cause is about accountability, agency, and ownership. It is an empathetic reframe of the common phrase "Don't be a victim," which is meant to empower but often triggers a defensive stance instead. When we use the language of being at cause, it takes what may be the same challenge someone felt victimized by and unlocks a new positive perspective. Seemingly small structural and language changes have a bigger impact than people realize. So does modeling the behavior you want to see. A big proponent of the "leaders go first" mindset, Brandt told us, "You always hear 'Do as I say, not as I do.' And that doesn't work in leadership and culture... Nothing will destroy it faster." (This reminds us of an old Marines adage marketing expert Tony Wells shared with us: "Leaders eat last," which relates directly to modeling leadership, humility, and values.[5]) She said some behaviors she's seen Schnuck model are his investments in culture, willingness to receive feedback, and candid communication style. It opens the door for everyone in the company to grow, connect, and resolve conflict peacefully. With this kind of dedication to people and humanity, we envision Schnuck Markets nourishing people's lives for many years to come.

What the Greatest Leaders Have in Common

While we love sharing a wide variety of tips, tools, and frameworks so you can tailor them to your needs, there is also a great deal of value in highlighting the patterns we've seen across companies and industries.

Conclusion

The most remarkable leaders we've met and worked with have commonalities across seven areas:

- *They have vision.* These leaders have the gumption to dream big, the foresight to envision future possibilities, and the fortitude to stay the course.

- *They have a "for all" mindset and bring humility into even the biggest leadership jobs.* They serve as a reminder to never forget where you came from or think you are better than anyone else.

- *They are driven by empathy.* This is often the impetus behind their vision.

- *They see culture as an indispensable pillar of strategy.* Remarkable leaders diligently nurture, refine, and grow its impact on their teams.

- *They are lifelong learners.* They surround themselves with good people and are willing to learn from the next generation. Whether you're reading this book the month it comes out or twenty years from now, the people behind you will always have something to teach you about inclusion, adaptability, and innovation.

- *They are great communicators and storytellers.* Great communication keeps everyone on the same page. These leaders are committed to developing creative solutions and multiple modes of disseminating key information.

- *They are servant leaders.* This means that they are focused on collaboration with a genuine, fundamental commitment to improving the lives of the people they lead, their clients and customers, and the communities they serve.

We may have come to the end of this chapter, and this book, but we know this is just the beginning for you and your culture design. It is our great hope that all of us will play a role in the future of business and the future for all. Lead with guts, brains, and heart. Know, do, and measure what matters in your company so you and your employees will be empowered to be at cause. Embrace what makes each of us human and get creative as you nail down solutions to the toughest dilemmas. And when it comes to celebrating progress in your organization, sweat the small stuff. Small moments are what make up your life. You've only got one. Make it count.

Notes

Introduction

1. Cody Corrall, Alyssa Stringer, and Kate Park, "A Comprehensive List of 2025 Tech Layoffs," *Tech Crunch*, March 26, 2025, https://techcrunch.com/2025/03/26/tech-layoffs-2025-list/.

2. Tony Wells, interview with authors, April 19, 2024; Dave Peacock, interview with authors, March 25, 2024.

3. Wells, interview.

4. Michelle MiJung Kim, *The Wake Up: Closing the Gap between Good Intentions and Real Change* (New York: Hachette Go, 2021), 28.

5. Kim, *The Wake Up*, 30.

Chapter 1

1. "Organically Grown Company Pioneers Groundbreaking Ownership Structure to Maintain Mission and Independence in Perpetuity," RSF Social Finance, July 9, 2019, https://rsfsocialfinance.org/2018/07/09/organically-grown-company-pioneers-groundbreaking-ownership-structure-to-maintain-mission-independence-in-perpetuity/.

2. Lee Wallace, interview with authors, April 5, 2024.

3. Brenna Davis, interview with authors, March 29, 2024.

4. "Employee Productivity vs. Hours Worked: Guidance for Managers," ActivTrak, May 7, 2024, https://www.activtrak.com/blog/employee-productivity-vs-hours-worked/.

5. Deborah Lovich, "Close Encounters of the Best Kind: Workplace 'Collisions,'" *Forbes*, September 15, 2021, https://www.forbes.com/sites/deborahlovich/2021/09/15/close-encounters-of-the-best-kind-workplace-collisions/.

6. "GLAAD Media Reference Guide—11th Edition," GLAAD, https://glaad.org/reference/.

7. "Black Friday," Patagonia, https://www.patagonia.com/black-friday.html.

Notes

8. Dave Peacock, interview with authors, March 25, 2024.
9. Tony Wells, interview with authors, April 19, 2024.

Chapter 2

1. Dave Peacock, interview with authors, March 25, 2024.
2. "Star Model," Galbraith Management Consultants, n.d., https://jaygalbraith.com/services/star-model/, accessed April 28, 2025.
3. Hermina Reicher, "Amazon's Tools: One Pages, Six Pages, and Backwards Press Release," LinkedIn, June 8, 2023, https://www.linkedin.com/pulse/amazons-tools-one-pager-six-backwards-press-release-hermina-reicher.
4. Lee Wallace, interview with authors, April 5, 2024.
5. Paul Butler, interview with authors, June 14, 2024.
6. Paul Butler, John Manfredi, and Peter Klein, *Think to Win: Unleashing the Power of Strategic Thinking* (New York: McGraw Hill Education, 2015), 181.
7. Christa Quarles, interview with authors, July 1, 2024.

Chapter 3

1. Jil Littlejohn Bostick, interview with authors, June 16, 2024.
2. Chris Argyris and Donald A. Schön, *Theory in Practice: Increasing Professional Effectiveness* (San Francisco: Jossey-Bass, 1974); Peter M. Senge, *The Fifth Discipline: The Art and Practice of the Learning Organization* (New York: Doubleday/Currency, 2006).
3. Sam Bright, interview with authors, September 6, 2024.
4. "Transparent," etymonline, n.d., https://www.etymonline.com/word/transparent, accessed April 28, 2025.
5. James Surowiecki, "What's Gone Wrong at Boeing," *The Atlantic*, January 15, 2024, https://www.theatlantic.com/ideas/archive/2024/01/boeing-737-max-corporate-culture/677140/.
6. Chris Isidore, "Boeing Was Once Known for Safety and Engineering. But Critics Say an Emphasis on Profits Changed That," CNN, January 30, 2024, https://www.cnn.com/2024/01/30/business/boeing-history-of-problems/index.html.
7. Bill George, "Why Boeing's Problems with the 737 MAX Began More Than 25 Years Ago," *Working Knowledge*, January 24, 2024, https://hbswk.hbs.edu/item/why-boeings-problems-with-737-max-began-more-than-25-years-ago.
8. "First Year Applicants—Essays," Sarah Lawrence College, https://www.sarahlawrence.edu/admission/apply/first-year.html#acc-312-essays.
9. "We're Guided by Our Core Beliefs," Truss, https://truss.works/values.
10. Everett Harper, interview with authors, February 7, 2025.
11. Timothy Escamilla, interview with authors, September 12, 2024.
12. Carla Vernón, interview with authors, April 15, 2024.
13. Bright, interview.

Notes

Chapter 4

1. Sam Bright, interview with authors, September 6, 2024.
2. J. Bruce Harreld and Christian Karega, "Jamba Juice (A)," Case 713-536 (Boston: Harvard Business School, 2013); and "Jamba Juice (B)," Case 713-537 Supplement (Boston: Harvard Business School, 2013).
3. B. W. Tuckman, "Developmental Sequence in Small Groups," *Psychological Bulletin* 63, no. 6 (1965): 384–399, https://doi.org/10.1037/h0022100; Cynthia D. Scott and Dennis T. Jaffe, "Survive and Thrive in Times of Change," *Training and Development Journal* 42, no. 4 (1988): 25–27, https://assets.td.org/m/31bbab75e4c745e2/original/Survive-and-Thrive-in-Times-of-Change.pdf. Elisabeth Kübler-Ross created the change curve in her analysis of the stages of grief, but it has often been adapted to help understand change in organizations. See, for example, "Understanding the Kübler-Ross Change Curve in the Workplace," Indeed, March 26, 2025, https://www.indeed.com/career-advice/career-development/change-curve.
4. Peter Senge, *The Fifth Discipline: The Art and Practice of the Learning Organization* (New York: Doubleday, 2006).
5. Matthew Stevens and Tracy Cioffi, interview with authors, August 28, 2024.
6. "Annual Update 2023: The Actions We Live By," Bay Club (Vimeo), November 14, 2022, https://vimeo.com/770962435.

Chapter 5

1. Sam Bright, interview with authors, September 6, 2024.
2. Bill Schaninger, Bryan Hancock, and Emily Field, *Power to the Middle: Why Managers Hold the Keys to the Future of Work* (Boston: Harvard Business Review Press, 2023).
3. Dirk Hampson, interview with authors, August 24, 2024.
4. Timothy Escamilla, interview with authors, September 12, 2024.
5. Dave Peacock, interview with authors, March 25, 2024.
6. Katrina Brooker, "Jim Kilts Is an Old-School Curmudgeon. Nothing Could Be Better for Gillette," *Fortune*, December 30, 2002, https://money.cnn.com/magazines/fortune/fortune_archive/2002/12/30/334571/index.htm.

Chapter 6

1. David Satterwhite, interview with authors, February 4, 2025.
2. "Insights," Culture Amp, https://www.cultureamp.com/science/insights.
3. "The Definition of a Great Workplace," Great Place to Work, https://greatplacetowork.me/trust-model/.
4. "About the Organizational Culture Assessment Instrument," OCAI Online, https://www.ocai-online.com/about-the-Organizational-Culture-Assessment-Instrument-OCAI.

5. Timothy Escamilla, interview with authors, September 12, 2024.
6. Adapted from frameworks from GlobalEdg LLC; and Paul Butler, John Manfredi, and Peter Klein, *Think to Win: Unleashing the Power of Strategic Thinking* (New York: McGraw-Hill Education, 2015).
7. Dave Peacock, interview with authors, March 25, 2024.

Conclusion

1. Dirk Hampson, interview with authors, August 28, 2024.
2. Todd Schnuck and Stacy Brandt, interview with authors, September 26, 2024.
3. Schnuck and Brandt, interview.
4. Schnuck and Brandt, interview.
5. Tony Wells, interview with authors, April 19, 2024.

Index

About Me tool, 94–95
action-learning teams
   employee resource groups, 61–62
   and iteration, 101–102
   STAR model, 50–52
"actions we live by," 107–108
action-taking step, in STAR model, 48, 50
active listening, 23–25
adhocracy, 140
Advantage Solutions, 3
   decision-making at, 46
   empathetic leadership at, 41, 124
   inspiration at, 151
AI (artificial intelligence), 2, 58–59, 159
Alludo, 60
Amazon, 55, 57
analysis, data, 144–147
annual reviews, 140–141
archaeological dig metaphor
   company symbols, 31–33
   departmental surveys, 38–39
   filtering tools, 47–55
   HR processes, 33–35
   internal documentation, 38
   interviewing managers and team members, 39
   mapping results, 35–43
   presenting findings, 40–43
   rewards, 29–30
   rituals, 28–29
   roundtables, town halls, and one-on-ones, 39–40
   say/do gap, 30–31
   written artifacts, 26–28
Argyris, Chris, 75
artificial intelligence (AI), 2, 58–59, 159
assessment of situation step, in STAR model, 48–49
auditing culture. *See* culture audit

Bay Club, 107–109, 123
behaviors lever, 148–149
"Be here now" motto, 168
being present, 168
belonging, sense of, 158–159
Benson, John, 115
"Be the best" value, 72
Blend plan, Jamba Juice, 54–55, 97–99
Block, Terry, 164
Boeing, 81–82
Bolthouse Fresh Foods
   clarifying roles and responsibilities at, 88
   communication at, 86
   empathetic leadership at, 123–124
branding, 31–33
Brandt, Stacy, 167–169
breakpoints, in organization size, 60–61
Bright, Sam, 76–77, 80, 87, 94–95, 97, 113, 143

Index

building for future. *See* future, building for
Butler, Paul, 59, 147–148

camaraderie, in Great Places to Work trust model, 138
capabilities lever, 148
cause, being at, 169
CECP (Chief Executives for Corporate Purpose) Summit, 17–18, 71
celebratory rituals, 29, 162–163
Center for Intentional Leadership, 168
change, implementing
    change levers, 59–60
    and crisis management, 79–83
    documentation in, 88
    and iteration, 104–107
    Jamba Juice, 70–71
    legal and compliance challenges, 83–86
    models of, 105
    overcoming resistance to, 75–79
    role of communication in, 86–87
    role of feedback in, 70–71
    Winnebago Industries, 71–75
Chief Executives for Corporate Purpose (CECP) Summit, 17–18, 71
childlore, 161
Chronus, 134–135
Cioffi, Tracy, 107
clan (collaborate) culture, 140
collaboration, Winnebago principle of unparalleled, 72
collecting data. *See* data collection
"command-and-control" culture, 60
communication
    active listening, 23–25
    collecting feedback, 75–77
    design thinking questions, 20–21
    expressing vulnerability, 21–23, 76
    feedback and iteration, 100–102
    importance of repetition, 62
    indirect listening, 21
    leading questions, 20–21
    making space for feedback, 62–63
    mapped archaeological dig for, 37
    one-on-one listening, 39–40
    open-ended questions, 20, 38, 64, 152
    open-mindedness, 19–20, 100–102
    role in good leadership, 170
    role in implementing change, 75–79, 86–87
    roundtables, 39–40
    shared language, 63, 75
    sharing results of culture audit, 63–64
    "speaking from the left-hand column" tool, 63, 75–76
    tailoring message to different roles and functions, 62–63
    town halls, 39–40
    and trust-building, 77
    yes/no questions, 20–21
CommunityGO initiative, 72
company culture. *See* culture; culture audit; culture design; Culture Design Lab
company symbols, 31–33
compete culture, 140
compliance issues, in culture change process, 83–86
    marketing amid social media censorship, 85–86
    Sarah Lawrence College, 83–84
    Truss digital services firm, 84–85
Conant, Doug, 22
continuum of change. *See* change, implementing
control culture, 140
cost-versus-value decisions for technology, 121
Covid-19 pandemic
    and Bay Club, 109
    and Google Play, 80

Index

Krista White's work experience during, 119
create culture, 140
creative tension, 106
credibility, in Great Places to Work trust model, 137
crisis management, 79–83
cross-functional groups
    action-learning teams, 50–52, 61–62, 101–102
    Far Niente, 161–162
    Jamba Juice, 50–51
cross-sectional data analysis, 145
cultural levers, 148–150
culture. *See also* reality of culture, defining
    challenges facing companies, 2
    consequences of weak, 2
    defined, 3
    importance of, 1–2
    intentional approach to, 2–3
    say/do gap in, 5–6
    supporting longevity of, 161–163
Culture Amp software, 135–137
culture audit, 25–40
    company symbols, 31–33
    departmental surveys, 38–39
    filtering tools, 47–55
    HR processes, 33–35
    internal documentation, 38
    interviewing managers and team members, 39
    mapping results, 35–43
    presenting findings, 40
    rewards, 29–30
    rituals, 28–29
    roundtables, town halls, and one-on-ones, 39–40
    say/do gap, 30–31
    written artifacts, 26–28
Culture Design (framework)
    creation of, 4–6
    defined, 6

Leaders Define the Reality step, 47
Leaders Empathize step, 18, 43
road map to design culture change, 61–64
culture design (process/concept)
    cyclical nature of, 151
    design thinking process, 6–8
    guiding questions, 13
    importance of, 2
    intentional approach to, 3
    role of patience in, 11
Culture Design Lab
    founding of, 3–5
    lifeline exercise, 94–95
    measuring progress, 132–133
culture problem statement, 59
curiosity, role in empathetic leadership, 19–21

data analysis, 144–147
data collection, 137–144
    comprehensive tools, 137–138
    low-tech tools, 141–142
    qualitative measurement, 143–144
    self-evaluation frameworks, 138–141
data visualization, 59, 145–147
Davis, Brenna, 27
decision-making
    cost-versus-value decisions, 121
    human-centered, 159–160
    integrative approach to, 46
defining reality. *See* reality of culture, defining
DEI initiatives, 83–84
demographic data, 133, 135–136
departmental surveys, 38–39
disruptions, external, 79–83
documentation
    codifying and scaling change with, 88
    internal, reviewing, 38
    reviewing written artifacts, 26–28
Dole Fresh Foods, 165

Index

"Don't let perfect be the enemy of good" principle, 82
"Do the right thing" value, 72, 116–117
"Do what matters" principle, 64, 80. *See also* change, implementing; iteration
Drucker, Peter, 69
Duolingo, 33

"each one teach one" philosophy, 118
empathetic leadership, 17–43. *See also* culture audit
   active listening, 23–25
   at Advantage Solutions, 41–42
   at Bay Club, 123
   at Bolthouse Fresh Foods, 123–124
   expressing vulnerability, 21–23
   general discussion, 40–43
   humility and curiosity in, 19–21
   people-first leadership style, 46
   storytelling series driving, 42
   at USAA, 42–43
employee net promoter score (eNPS), 134–135
employees
   knowing when to let move on, 78–79
   relationship with leadership at Winnebago, 73–74
engagement measurement tools, 137–144
   annual reviews, 140–141
   comprehensive tools, 137–138
   engagement surveys, 134, 136, 143–144
   Gallup Q12, 137
   Great Places to Work surveys, 137–138
   low-tech, 141–142
   Organizational Culture Assessment Instrument, 140–141
   qualitative measurement, 143–144
   self-evaluation frameworks, 138–141

engagement scores, 135
eNPS (employee net promoter score), 134–135
enterprise-wide surveys, 134
entry-level employees
   changing view of, 122–123
   importance of engaging with, 119
Escamilla, Timothy, 86, 88, 123–124, 160, 164–165
"exceptional experience" principle, 72
external disruptions, 79–83

FAA (Federal Aviation Administration), 81
fairness, in Great Places to Work trust model, 138
Far Niente Winery, 115–118
   cross-functional groups, 161–162
   "Do the right thing" value, 116–117
   "each one teach one" philosophy, 118
   employee recognition, 162
   fostering internal opportunities for growth, 117–118
   human-centered decision-making, 160
   rewarding current employees, 117
Federal Aviation Administration (FAA), 81
feedback
   at Gillette, 126
   honest and respectful, 142
   importance of, 86–87
   and iteration, 100–102
   making space for, 62–63
   role in implementing change, 70–71, 75–77
Field, Emily, 114
filtering tools
   future-back method, 52–55
   STAR model, 47–52
Floyd, George, 10
"for all" mindset, 138, 170

Index

FormFactor, 102
Fourth Industrial Revolution, 128
frontline workers
   changing view of, 122–123
   engaging with, 119
future, building for, 155–171
   commonalities of great leaders, 169–171
   human-centered decision-making, 159–160
   intergenerational collaboration, 156–158
   job creation, 156
   "Know Why You Keep Going" exercise, 160
   leader role models, 164–166
   mentorship, 156
   overview, 155–156
   and quiet quitting, 159
   Schnuck Markets, 166–169
   sense of belonging, 158–159
   supporting cultural longevity, 161–163
future-back method, 52–55

Galbraith, Jay R., 47–48
Gallup Q12, 137
"Game Film" review, 168
gauging impact step, STAR model, 48, 50
generational differences, 156–158, 159
Gen Z, 2, 157, 159
Gillette, 52, 125–126
GLAAD, 33
GlobalEdg, 147–148
global events, disruptive, 79–83
goal(s) step, in STAR model, 48–49
good vs. perfect, 82
Google Forms, 141
Google Play
   bidirectional empathy at, 94–95
   collecting qualitative data at, 143–144

communication at, 87
culture on large teams at, 113
trust-building at, 77
great leaders, commonalities of, 169–171
Great Places to Work surveys, 137–138

Hammersmith, Kelli, 41
Hampson, Dirk, 115–118, 159, 161, 164
Hancock, Bryan, 114
Happe, Michael, 71
hard skills, 29
Harper, Everett, 84
health-care metaphor, 132
hierarchy culture, 140
hiring data, 135
Honest Company
   "Ask Carla Anything" listening sessions, 87
   company symbols, 31–32
   rituals, 28, 162
HR (human resources)
   processes of, reviewing, 33–35
   strategies of, reimagining and redesigning, 63–64
human-centered decision-making, 159–160
humility
   role in empathetic leadership, 19–21
   and vulnerability, 22

images, branding, 33
impact, gauging, in STAR model, 48, 50
implementing change. *See* change, implementing
individual level, cultural levers at, 148–149
information lever, 150
intentional leadership, 168–169
intergenerational collaboration, 156–158
internal documentation, reviewing, 38

Index

interviews
    HR strategies for, 64
    of managers and team members, 39
    practicing humility and curiosity in, 19–21
iteration, 91–110
    action-learning teams, 101–102
    at Bay Club, 107–109
    and change, 104–107
    and feedback, 100–102
    at Google Play, 94–95, 97
    at Jamba Juice, 97–99
    by James D. White, 95–104
    lifeline exercise, 95–97
    overview, 91–94
    strategy and culture design, 100–104

Jaffe, Dennis, 105
JambaGo, 54
Jamba Juice
    action-learning teams, 50–52
    Blend plan, 54–55, 97–99
    collecting feedback from stakeholders, 70
    crisis management, 82–83
    future-back method, 54–55
    iteration at, 97–99
    STAR model use at, 47–48, 50–51
    town halls, 40
job creation, 156
Jobs, Steve, 108, 164

Kiki For The Future app, 4, 6, 25, 45–46, 58
Kilts, Jim, 125–126, 164
Kim, Michelle MiJung, 10–11
Klein, Peter, 60
knowing what matters, 7. *See also* empathetic leadership; reality of culture, defining

"Know Why You Keep Going" exercise, 160

leaders. *See also* future, building for; iteration; progress, measuring
    commonalities of great leaders, 169–171
    intentional leadership, 168–169
    key, enlisting for culture transformation, 63
    lineage of, 164–166
    relationship with employees at Winnebago, 73–74
Leaders Define the Reality step, in Culture Design framework, 47. *See also* reality of culture, defining
"leaders eat last" concept, 169
Leaders Empathize step, in Culture Design framework, 18, 43. *See also* empathetic leadership
"leaders go first" mindset, 168
leadership lever, 148
leading questions, 20–21
Lee, Megan Myungwon, 17–18
legal issues in culture change process, 83–86
    marketing amid social media censorship, 85–86
    Sarah Lawrence College, 83–84
    Truss digital services firm, 84–85
LGBTQIA+ community, 4, 45–46, 58
lifeline exercise, 95–97
lifelong learning, 170
listening skills
    active listening, 23–25
    "Ask Carla Anything" listening sessions, 87
    at Google Play, 97
    indirect listening, 21
    one-on-one listening, 39–40
    roundtables, 39–40
    town halls, 39–40

Index

Littlejohn Bostick, Jil, 71, 72–74
live 360 process, 168
logos, 32–33

"management by walking around" method, 124
managers
   action-learning teams, 50–51
   addressing needs of, 118–122, 128
   challenges facing, 114
   interviewing in culture audit, 39
Manfredi, John, 60
mapping culture audit results, 35–43
market (compete) culture, 140
McDonnell Douglas, 82
measuring what matters, 7. *See also* progress, measuring
"melting pot vs. salad" metaphor, 74
Member Services Day, USAA, 42–43
mentorship
   Chronus, 134–135
   fostering intergenerational collaboration, 156
metrics. *See* progress, measuring
Meyer, Danny, 45
middle managers
   action-learning teams, 50–51
   addressing needs of, 118–122, 128
   challenges facing, 114
millennials, 157, 159
"mission moment," USAA, 42
mission statement, 26
Moments That Matter, 41–42
Morris-Thornton, Pamela, 41

narrative, as culture design tool, 163
Nestlé Purina, 52, 63, 75, 127, 164
Netflix, 53
Nickel, Gil, 116, 164

Obama, Barack, 164
OCAI (Organizational Culture Assessment Instrument), 140–141
OGC (Organically Grown Company), 27, 29
one-on-one listening, 39–40
on-site vs. remote work debate, 73
open-ended questions
   departmental surveys, 38
   interviews, 20, 64
   and survey fatigue, 152
open-mindedness
   around bidirectional communication, 101–102
   in interviewing, 19–20
OpenTable, 60
Organically Grown Company (OGC), 27, 29
organizational culture. *See* culture
Organizational Culture Assessment Instrument (OCAI), 140–141
organizational level, cultural levers at, 149–150

Patagonia, 33
Peace Coffee, 28, 59, 80–81, 162
Peacock, Dave, 3, 41, 46, 124, 151, 164, 165
people-first leadership style
   at Advantage Solutions, 46
   at Winnebago Industries, 71–73
people strategy, reimagining and redesigning, 63–64
permacrisis, 2
physical space, 32
plan, working the. *See* change, implementing
plan of action step, in STAR model, 48–49
policies and processes lever, 149–150
Power to the Middle (Schaninger, Hancock, and Field), 114

Index

present, being, 168
press release method, defining vision with, 55–58
pride, in Great Places to Work trust model, 138
prioritization tools
  future-back method, 52–55
  STAR model, 47–52
profit as motivation, 11–12
progress, measuring, 131–154
  choosing what to measure, 133–137
  cultural levers for, 148–150
  data analysis, 144–147
  data collection, 137–144
  demographic data, 133, 135–136
  engagement scores, 135
  hiring and promotion, 135
  implementing action plan, 147–151
  survey fatigue, 151–153
promotion data, 135
purpose
  identifying, 9–0
  why statement, 12–13
"Purpose and Persistence" conference, 17–18
"purposeful innovation" principle, 72
purpose statement, 26
"Put people first" value, 72

qualitative data measurement, 143–144
Quarles, Christa, 60–61
quarterly check-in templates, 140–141
quiet quitting, 159

Ravikant, Naval, 91
reality of culture, defining, 45–65
  and AI, 58–59
  and breakpoints, 60–61
  change levers, 59–60
  culture problem statement, 59
  data visualization tools, 59
  future-back method, 52–55
  press release method, 55–58
  road map to culture transformation, 61–64
  STAR model, 47–52
recognition, 150. *See also* rewards
relational, being, 168–169
"relentless excellence" principle, 72
remote vs. on-site work debate, 73
resistance to change, overcoming, 75–79
  knowing when to let employees move on, 78–79
  by providing certainty, 86
  responding to sore spots, 76–77
  role of shared language in, 75–76
  with thoughtful communication, 77
respect, in Great Places to Work trust model, 138
rewards
  in culture audit, 29–30
  for growth-oriented behavior, 61
  rewards and recognition lever, 150
rituals
  celebratory, 29, 162
  in culture audit, 28–29
  Honest Company, 28
  Peace Coffee, 28, 162
  vs. rewards, 29–30
road map to culture transformation, 61–64
  action-learning teams, 61
  effectively communicating plans, 62–63
  employee resource groups, 61–62
  enlisting key leaders, 63
  people strategy, reimagining and redesigning, 63–64
  steps of, 61
role models of leadership, 164–166
Roosevelt, F. D., 164
roundtables, 39–40

Index

Safeway, 52
"salad vs. melting pot" metaphor, 74
Sarah Lawrence College, 83–84
Satterwhite, David, 134–135
say/do gap
   checking for, 30–31
   effect on employee happiness, 2
   as framework for evaluations and survey questions, 143
   overview, 5–6
   role in qualitative measurement, 143
Schaninger, Bill, 114
Schnuck, Anna, 166
Schnuck, Don, 167
Schnuck, Todd, 167–168
Schnuck Markets, 166–169
Schön, Donald, 75
Scott, Aliza, 102
Scott, Cynthia, 105
self-evaluation frameworks, 138–141
   Chief Executives for Corporate Purpose, 140–141
   Krista White on, 139
   Organizational Culture Assessment Instrument, 139–140
Senge, Peter, 75–76, 106
sense of belonging, 158–159
servant leaders, 170–171
shared language, 63, 75
silos, 86
Slessor, Mike, 102
soft skills, 29
"speaking from the left-hand column" tool, 63, 75–76
sprint teams
   employee resource groups, 61–62
   and iteration, 101–102
   Jamba Juice, 50–52
standards, brand, 32–33
STAR (strategic thinking and results) model, 47–52
   action-learning teams, 50–52
   assessment of situation step, 48–49

gauging impact step, 48, 50
goal(s) step, 48–49
plan of action step, 48–49
questions to consider, 49–50
strategy step, 48, 49
taking action step, 48, 50
Stevens, Matthew, 123, 164. *See also* Bay Club
storytelling, 42
strategic thinking and results model. *See* STAR model
strategy, and culture design, 100–104
strategy step, STAR model, 48, 49
structure lever, 149
style guides, 32–33
Survey Monkey, 141
surveys
   departmental, 38–39
   engagement, 134, 136, 143–144
   enterprise-wide, 134
   Great Places to Work, 137–138
   survey fatigue, 151–153
Sustainable Food and Agriculture Perpetual Purpose Trust, 27
symbols, company, 31–33

taking action step, STAR model, 48, 50
task forces
   employee resource groups, 61–62
   and iteration, 101–102
   at Jamba Juice, 50–52
team building, 74
team members, interviewing in culture audit, 39
technology
   cost-versus-value decisions, 121
   using intentionally, 159
Think to Win (Butler, Manfredi, and Klein), 59–60
tomato war, OCG, 29
town halls, 39–40
Truss digital services firm, 84–85

Index

trust-building
  and communication, 77
  reducing anxiousness by providing certainty, 86
trust model, Great Places to Work, 137–138
Tuckman, Bruce, 105
Tyson, Bernard, 131

"unparalleled collaboration" principle, 72
Upwork, 80
USAA, 42–43

values statement, 26
Vernón, Carla, 28, 31–32, 87, 162, 165
videos, branding, 33
visualization, data, 59, 145–147
visual reminders, 163
voice notes, 142
vulnerability, expressing, 21–23

The Wake Up (Kim), 10
Wallace, Lee, 28, 59, 80–81
weak culture, dangers of, 2
Wells, Tony, 3, 5–6, 42–43, 143, 169
White, James (father), 166
White, James D.
  Blend plan at Jamba Juice, 97–99
  career background and approach to business, 3–4
  crisis management, 82–83
  on empathetic leadership, 22
  experiencing frontline reality, 114–115
  expressing vulnerability, 23, 76
  future-back method, 52–55
  at Gillette, 125
  leadership lineage, 165–166
  lifeline exercise, 95–97
  at Nestlé Purina, 126
  note-taking style, 8–9
  paper-and-pen method, 46–47
  respectful feedback, 142
  speech at CECP Summit, 17
  Stanford Distinguished Careers Institute fellow, 6
  town hall for Jamba Juice, 40
White, Krista
  active listening, 25
  benefits of international culture, 157–158
  career background and approach to business, 4
  design thinking process, 45–46
  grad school experience, 157–158
  importance of engaging with frontline workers, 119
  on iteration, 92
  leadership lineage, 166
  note-taking style, 9
  press release method, 56–58
  research for KiKi For The Future app, 25
  self-evaluation, 139
  UX design courses, 6
  value of understanding etymology of terms, 78
  work-life integration, 159
White, Rose Marie, 165–166
Whitehead, Mike, 168
why
  identifying, 9–12
  why statement, 12–13
Winnebago Industries, 71–75
working the plan. *See* change, implementing
work-life integration, 158–159
written artifacts, reviewing, 26–28

yes/no questions, 20, 21

Zero Day PT, USAA, 42–43

Acknowledgments

First, we would like to thank our family. James's wife, Rhonda, has played every role—business partner, marketing strategist, biggest supporter, and reader—at every stage. Through the years, we have come to appreciate our loved ones more than ever. James's father and Krista's Papa, James White Sr., reminds us to work hard, laugh hard, and remain optimistic through life's ups and downs. We thank our mother and Granny, Rose Marie White, who we know is with us still in spirit. Endless thanks to Brittany Jones-Kugel and Phillip Kugel, Cheryl and John Jones, Jasmine and Lisa White, and Taylor Shantz. Much like the Bay Club, we know family isn't only blood. James has been blessed to have the support and camaraderie of his childhood friends Steve Clerkley, Myron Gillmore, and John "Lefty" Beard for the past forty-plus years. He can't wait for many more years of laughter, concerts, and brotherhood. Krista won't name every friend who has encouraged her as she wrote this book because if she leaves someone out, she won't hear the end of it. Much love to her best friend, her longtime roommate, and her twin in another life, Keith Williams. This is all just like we planned.

Krista would like to thank the Sarah Lawrence creative writing community, whom she met while working on this book. The writers,

Acknowledgments

professors, and leaders she had the privilege of working with during her MFA program pushed her writing far past her comfort zone—and she's a better author, storyteller, and human for it. Thank you to Darcie Dennigan, Joseph Earl Thomas, Carolyn Ferrell, David Hollander, Garth Risk-Hallberg, Domenica Ruta, Meredith Talusan, Maddie Mori, and Paige Ackerson-Kiely.

Though there are only two names on the cover, it takes a village to publish a book. Thank you to our editor, Scott Berinato, for your sharp edits, your steadfast support of this project, and your collaboration throughout the entire process. We made a book! We are grateful to you, Julie Devoll, Felicia Sinusas, and the entire team at Havard Business Review Press for their partnership on *Culture Design*. We would also like to thank Jazmine Cable-Whitehurst for her research, input, and extremely organized spreadsheets. Your diligence does not go unnoticed.

We would like to thank the brilliant leaders whose wise feedback is reflected in these pages. Thank you to Joe Dworetzky, Jay Harris, Keith Meyer, and Pam Morris-Thornton, for reading early versions of this book and helping us polish our message. Thank you to our interviewees, Stacy Brandt, Daryl Brewster, Sam Bright, Paul Butler, Tracy Cioffi, Brenna Davis, Timothy Escamilla, Dirk Hampson, Everett Harper, Jil Littlejohn Bostick, Rebecca Marks, Dave Peacock, Christa Quarles, David Satterwhite, Todd Schnuck, Mike Slessor, Matthew Stevens, Carla Vernón, Lee Wallace, and Tony Wells. You taught us more than we could have imagined. Many thanks to Paul Witkay, the founder and CEO of the Alliance of Chief Executives, and the trailblazing leader who introduced us to several of the CEOs we interviewed.

Thank you to Mat Miller, Alana Whitman, and the team at Book-Highlight for your outstanding work to get this book to the audiences

Acknowledgments

who need it most. Thank you to Mark Fortier and the team at Fortier PR—your expertise on the PR front has helped us widen our reach.

We are also so grateful to you, our reader, who has made it all the way to the end. Thank you for your time and attention. We hope we have given you something you will carry with you.

About the Authors

James D. White is a transformational leader with more than thirty years of experience as a CEO and operating executive. He has overseen the evolution and growth of some of the world's most iconic brands in the consumer products, retail, and restaurant industries. As the former chair, president, and CEO of Jamba Juice, White led the successful turnaround and transformation of the company from a smoothie shop to a leading global healthy and active-lifestyle brand, and he has held senior executive roles at Safeway Stores, Gillette, Nestlé Purina PetCare, and Coca-Cola. James has become a sought-after board member over the last twenty years, serving on over twenty public and private company boards. He currently serves as chair of the board of directors of the Honest Company and as a member of the board of directors of CAVA Group, Schnuck Markets, Simply Good, Greenlight, and the Bay Club. In 2019, James cofounded Culture Design Lab, which works with CEOs and leaders to intentionally design high-performing, resilient company cultures and organizations. Throughout his career, James has demonstrated his commitment to designing culture and inclusive workplaces, and he is the cofounder and chair of the Director's Academy, a national nonprofit with a mission to identify, develop, and advance the next generation of corporate board leaders.

About the Authors

Krista White is a multigenre nonfiction author and fiction writer. As a cofounder of Culture Design Lab, her work focuses on research, in-depth interviews, and harnessing her writing and storytelling skills to craft powerful narratives. She collaborates with the team to weave their incredible combined experiences into digestible communications, reports, and publications for Culture Design Lab's clients. In addition to her work at Culture Design Lab, Krista has consulted with individuals and companies on their strategies for intentional culture design, inclusion, and racial justice. She is also the founder and CEO of Kiki For The Future, a platform for LGBTQIA+ sex education, and recently graduated with her MFA in creative writing (fiction) at Sarah Lawrence College. All of her work ultimately centers around her values of liberation, connection, and joy.